Financial Wisdom For Financial Freedom

Practical Financial Stewardship

Dr. Chonta T. A. Haynes

Copyright © 2017 by Dr. Chonta T. A. Haynes.

ISBN: 978-0-9991733-0-5   eBook

ISBN: 978-0-9991733-1-2   Spiral bound/ Paperback

All rights reserved. No portion of this eBook may be reproduced, stored in a retrieval system, or transmitted in any form or by any means – electronic, mechanical, photocopy, recording, scanning, or other – except for brief quotations in critical reviews or articles, without the prior written permission of the copyright owner.

Unless otherwise indicated, all Scriptural quotations are from the *King James Version* of the Bible.

Scriptural references marked NIV are taken from the *Holy Bible*, New International Version ®NIV ® Copyright © 1973, 1978, 1984 by the International Bible Society. Used by permission of Zondervan Publishing House. All rights reserved.

Scriptural references marked NAS are taken from the *Holy Bible*, the NEW AMERICAN STANDARD BIBLE®, Copyright © 1960, 1962, 1963, 1971, 1972, 1973, 1975, 1977, 1995 by The Lockman Foundation. Used by permission.

Scripture quotations marked NLT are taken from the Holy Bible, New Living Translation, Copyright ©1996. Used by permission of Tyndale House Publishers, Inc., Wheaton, Illinois 60189. All rights reserved.

This book was printed in the United States of America.

To order additional copies in any format, contact:

Heart 2 Heart Truth Ministries, LLC

1-813-986-9660 or 1-813-299-2742

www.H2HTruth.org

www.ChontaHaynes.com

Table of Contents

Introduction	5
Chapter 1: Your Financial Mindset	7
God's Design	7
Money Facts	8
Goal Setting	11
Chapter 2: Banking/ Credit	15
Bank Accounts	16
Basics of Credit	19
Improving Your Scores	21
Chapter 3: Budgeting	23
God's Budget	28
Financial Fitness Assessment	30
Financial Game Plan	31
Spending Plan	32
Chapter 4: Saving/ Debt Reduction	34
Savings Plan	34
Debt's Dilemma	36
Reducing Debt	38
Chapter 5: Investing/ Net Worth	41
Investing Basics	41
Net Worth Calculations	42
Conclusion and Next Steps	44

Appendix

- Websites — 46
- Goals — 48
- Worksheets
  - Budget — 50
  - Bill Paying Calendar — 52
  - Balancing Your Check Book — 53
  - Net Worth — 54
- Examples
  - Budget — 55
  - Net Worth — 57
- Setting Goals & Sample Statements — 59
- Managing Debt & Credit — 59
- Maintaining a Good Credit Rating — 61
- Bankruptcy — 62
- Mortgage Basics — 64
- Practical Financial Stewardship Study — 67

Dedication

For my family: by marriage- Eric, Aryn, * , and Aaliyah; by birth- Mom (MaryAnne Andrews) and Erik Andrews; my extended family – you know who you are; and those to come – All who join me in partnership for abundant living.

Introduction

Where I am today is not where I started...

I wasn't born with a silver spoon in my mouth. I don't look like the environment I grew up in. My move to a place of financial independence and a comfortable space is a result of following the principles God ordained, and YOU CAN TOO!

I grew up with both parents until I was 13. We were content financially because as children we didn't know any better. My brother and I had no idea what was lacking. As far as we were concerned we had all that we ever needed or desired. The reality hit just last year. As I went back to my home I recognized that the financial support from the parent that left wasn't offered. When one parent is left holding all the responsibility for the finances, there is generally a shortfall. Living paycheck to paycheck lifestyle and having more month than money should not be the norm and is not God's design. Those of us who grew up in an environment that wasn't ideal financially tend to show it in our actions. I am a saver. I am always looking for a deal, and I am frugal. I enjoy quality products but still look for a savings. My best friends are Clarence & Clarissa (clearance) and Sally (sale). These are the first locations I look for in any store. I am a product of my environment yet I don't have the same state of mind. I am not content to remain lacking but I want all of the abundant life Jesus died to give me.

God's word tells us that prosperity is promised and our favor crown can easily be adjusted. The Word teaches us much about money; how it should be used; the importance of saving and giving; the benefits and the detriments. This writing is designed to help put into perspective what the Word says and how it should be practically put into action. The goal is to help you become financially fit and to develop a plan to reach an abundant place where your finances are concerned, then turn around and sow a seed to help someone else. So let's begin with practical financial wisdom for financial freedom as you soar to higher levels.

As you proceed through the chapters you will:

- ❖ Get a clear understanding and encouragement on what God's desire is for your financial freedom
- ❖ Set goals and dream of where you want to be
- ❖ Determine where to keep your money so you can use it wisely to pay for products and services and save
- ❖ Discover the benefits of a good credit score and learn what actions can help you improve yours
- ❖ Create a budget so that you come out of debt and move to financial freedom

- ❖ Develop a financial game plan to go from your current status to one more desirable
- ❖ Develop a spending plan so expenses don't exceed your income
- ❖ Develop a savings plan to reach family goals and future legacy goals
- ❖ Create a debt reduction plan, if necessary
- ❖ Begin investing so your money works for you and not you for your money

Thank you for allowing God's word to bring you to a place of financial peace as you journey through these pages. Let's begin….

"As a man thinks in his heart, so is he" – Proverbs 23:7a

Chapter 1: Your Financial Mindset

Are you ready to wash your mind from all of the wrong thoughts? Starting with what we think and how we think about money is necessary. If our focus and faith is in the money then we have already lost the battle. The Bible declares that money is fleeting; it is here today and gone tomorrow. We can't depend on the value, the abundance or what money can buy yet we need money to live in today's culture/economic system.

Jesus came that we might have an abundant life (John 10:10) and that means we need enough money to take care of our needs and then some. Does it mean that I haven't arrived unless the money is overflowing? Does it mean that I am defined by how much I have in the bank? The answer of course to both questions is NO. We use money but we shouldn't allow money to control us or use it to control others. Money is for our benefit in order to live a life that is pleasing. How that is defined is up to you.

A renewal of the mind is in order. Money is a means to obtain the necessities and luxuries of life. When we handle it properly life is easier. Our worth and value as an individual is not determined by how much money we have; it is defined by God.

God's Design

So does God require that I should be broke? The answer is a thousand times NO. We are called to be good stewards. A steward is one who manages the affairs of another. You didn't create money. You also don't have the ability in yourself to make money without the assistance of God. Can you breathe if that divine ability was removed? Would you have strength to complete your tasks at work if God didn't supply it? Could you even read without sight or comprehend without your brain? What we have then ultimately belongs to God (Psalm 24:1). The question becomes, how are you handling what God has given you?

God's desire for our management of money is clearly defined as you read from Genesis to Revelation. The gold is hidden throughout this book for you but all of the treasure isn't here. I encourage you to dig for yourself. God has a game plan for your budget, your savings, your investing and your overall improvement of your stewardship. All of these will be discussed but the overall design is for YOU to be an example. Be the ambassador that you were called and destined to be. Determine now to change what needs to change in order that you can be a light to those around you. Guide them after you have gotten your house in order. Believe and know ...YOU CAN DO THIS! AND YOU'LL BE A BLESSING TO OTHERS!

Money Facts

As reported by government data in 2015, 80 % of Americans are living above their means and are in debt. 24% -28% carry balances on a credit card averaging over $15,000 per household. The average mortgage debt is over $156,000 and the average student loan debt is $35,000. The debt clock for the US exceeds a number we cannot wrap our mind around. Consumer debt alone is over $3.34 trillion dollars. We can't truly imagine owing even the daily interest. Yet mismanagement of funds isn't the root of the problem; our thinking is the problem. Wanting today what you can't afford and not willing to wait creates indebtedness. Wisdom counts the cost before and is willing to say no if the cost is too high (Proverbs 13:11). Many today have a sense of entitlement; someone owes them. The truth of the matter is that at birth no one hired us nor signed a contract to say that we would get any amount of money for just breathing. What we have or earn is up to us to put in the sweat equity necessary to live and give at the level we desire.

Consider these Biblically based truths:

A good man leaves an inheritance for his children's children (Proverbs 13:22) so don't plan to spend it all.

As a good steward you should pay workers (Deuteronomy 24:10-17) without hesitation.

Co-signing leads to trouble (Proverbs 11:15, 17:18, 22:26, 6:1-5) beware and don't do it.

Debt should be repaid (Psalm 37:21; Leviticus 19:23; Exodus 22:14) therefore make a plan and have the mindset to pay for what you purchase.

Ideally you should owe no one (Deuteronomy 15:6, 28:12; Proverbs 22:7; Romans 13:8) therefore make another plan to be debt free.

Money can be corrupted (items rot or decay) (James 5:2) therefore beware.

Money can be hurtful (Ecclesiastes 5:13-14), enslaving (Proverbs 22:7) and unsatisfying (Ecclesiastes 5:10, 4:8) don't allow it to put you in bondage.

Money can make you lazy (Luke 12:13) so be mindful.

Money is choking (Matthew 13:22; Luke 8:14) so don't give it first place; it will steal those things most important to you.

Money is deceitful (Matthew 13:22) so don't trust in money.

Money is fleeting (Proverbs 23:5; Revelation 18:16-17) it shouldn't be counted on but used wisely.

Money is temporary (Proverbs 27:24), uncertain (1 Timothy 6:17) and perishable (Jeremiah 48:36) so make wise investments today.

The love of money is destructive (1 Timothy 6:10; Proverbs 15:27) so love God and use money.

You are blessed to be a blessing (Genesis 12:2) so don't keep it all to yourself.

The rich young ruler (Matthew 19:16-25; Mark 10:17-25) when he came to Jesus thought he had done everything necessary to get into heaven. When Jesus told him to sell everything he had, the Bible declares he went away sad because he had great possessions. Jesus said it is hard for a rich man to get into heaven and closer examination shows what prevented him; it was the trust in riches. Money is useful and God as our abundant supplier, giving us all sufficiency, wants to bless us but our trust should remain in Him and not the money or the material gain.

Riches can lead to these characteristics so **AVOID** them as you move to financial freedom:

Denying God (Proverbs 30:8-9 NKJV) - *"Remove falsehood and lies far from me; Give me neither poverty nor riches. Feed me with the food allotted to me; Lest I be full and deny You, And say, "Who is the LORD?" Or lest I be poor and steal, And profane the name of my God.*

Forgetting God (Deuteronomy 8:11-17 NKJV) – *"Beware that you do not forget the LORD your God by not keeping His commandments, His judgments, and His statutes which I command you today, lest—when you have eaten and are full, and have built beautiful houses and dwell in them; and when your herds and your flocks multiply, and your silver and your gold are multiplied, and all that you have is multiplied; when your heart is lifted up, and you forget the LORD your God who brought you out of the land of Egypt, from the house of bondage; who led you through that great and terrible wilderness, in which were fiery serpents and scorpions and thirsty land where there was no water; who brought water for you out of the flinty rock; who fed you in the wilderness with manna, which your fathers did not know, that He might humble you and that He might* *test you, to do you good in the end— then you say in your heart, 'My power and the might of my hand have gained me this wealth."*

- **Forsaking God** (Deuteronomy 32:15 ESV) - *"But Jeshurun grew fat, and kicked; you grew fat, stout, and sleek; then he forsook God who made him and scoffed at the Rock of his salvation.*

- **Oppression** (James 2:6 NKJV) – *"But you have dishonored the poor man. Do not the rich oppress you and drag you into the courts?*

- **Pride** (Ezekiel 28:5 NKJV) – *"By your great wisdom in trade you have increased your riches, And your heart is lifted up because of your riches"*

- **Rebelling against God** (Nehemiah 9:25-26 NIV) – *"They captured fortified cities and fertile land; they took possession of houses filled with all kinds of good things, wells already dug, vineyards, olive groves and fruit trees in abundance. They ate to the full and were well-nourished; they reveled in your great goodness. "But they were disobedient and rebelled against you; they put your law behind their backs. They killed your prophets, who had admonished them in order to turn them back to you; they committed awful blasphemies.*

- **Rudeness** (Proverbs 18:23 NIV) – *"A poor man pleads for mercy, but a rich man answers harshly."*

- **Violence** (Micah 6:12 NIV) – *"Her rich men are violent; her people are liars and their tongues speak deceitfully."*

God's design is to bless you so that you not only have bread for food but that you will have seed to sow (2 Corinthians 9:10). Don't consume all that you have or you won't have anything to give (sow) into anyone else. The truth of God's word brings light.

Let's start with a clear understanding of what the Bible says about money, its advantages and its detriments so that we use it effectively.

Goal Setting

Are you ready to dream?

Not small dreams of looking at what someone else has but dreaming your own dream. What is in your heart? What do you wish you had? Where do you want to go? What dream do you want to accomplish? I challenge you not to think small but reach for the moon. Develop a vision board. You can list your desires or you can cut out pictures to represent those aims. You can use the template that follows or the one in the appendix. However you decide to physically show yourself and the world what you desire, just do it. As we begin this journey to financial freedom it is imperative that you set goals so that you will achieve them. It has been noted that if you fail to plan, you plan to fail. In most instances if you set a realistic goal you will then create steps to achieve it. The Bible says it this way, where there is no vision, the people perish (Proverbs 29:18 a).

You should determine goals in at least 3 separate categories: financial dreams; family goals; and future legacy goals. The reason you set these is so that they are a vision for your future and you can achieve them. This is your "Why". Why you start the journey. Why living where you are now isn't sufficient or acceptable. Why you'll plan for a house and invest. It's the "Why" you set up a savings account and college fund. It's the goal that creates the plan to get you to retirement. It's your reason to proceed.

What is the major issue regarding your finances? Are you encumbered with debt? Are you stressed by your credit score? Is there too much month for your money? Are you saving for a large purchase? What ultimately would you like to accomplish? Take the time to identify where you want to go. Know that you aren't in this alone and most goals are achievable. Each step as you go thru the chapters in this book will align your finances so that your goals can be reached. Believe there is nothing you can't accomplish!

God's desire is that we prosper and be in good health even as our soul prospers (3 John 2) so we will start with meditating on the blessings from God in this area. Look back over the Biblically based truths previously mentioned. Meditate on them daily and pray this blessing until your mindset is in line with God's design.

God, bless us and keep us, make Your face to shine upon us and be gracious to us. In this financially volatile world we need You to be a shield of protection. Build a hedge around our resources. Guard us from the devourer and ourselves. You are the giver of every good and perfect gift and we acknowledge You as our provider. You promised to do exceeding abundantly above what we hope, ask or think. You declared that if we would seek Your Kingdom first, all things would be added to us. Show us the way to live according to Your Word. We need you to give us dreams of the abundant living You promised and then exceed that expectation. You are our Jehovah Jireh and there is nothing that You cannot supply. There is no mountain of impossibility You cannot remove. There is no debt too great and no credit too bad that You cannot fix. Our desire is to have our financial house in order and for You to be pleased. As your child we receive all that You have for us. We ask all these blessings in the mighty name of Jesus. AMEN

Goals

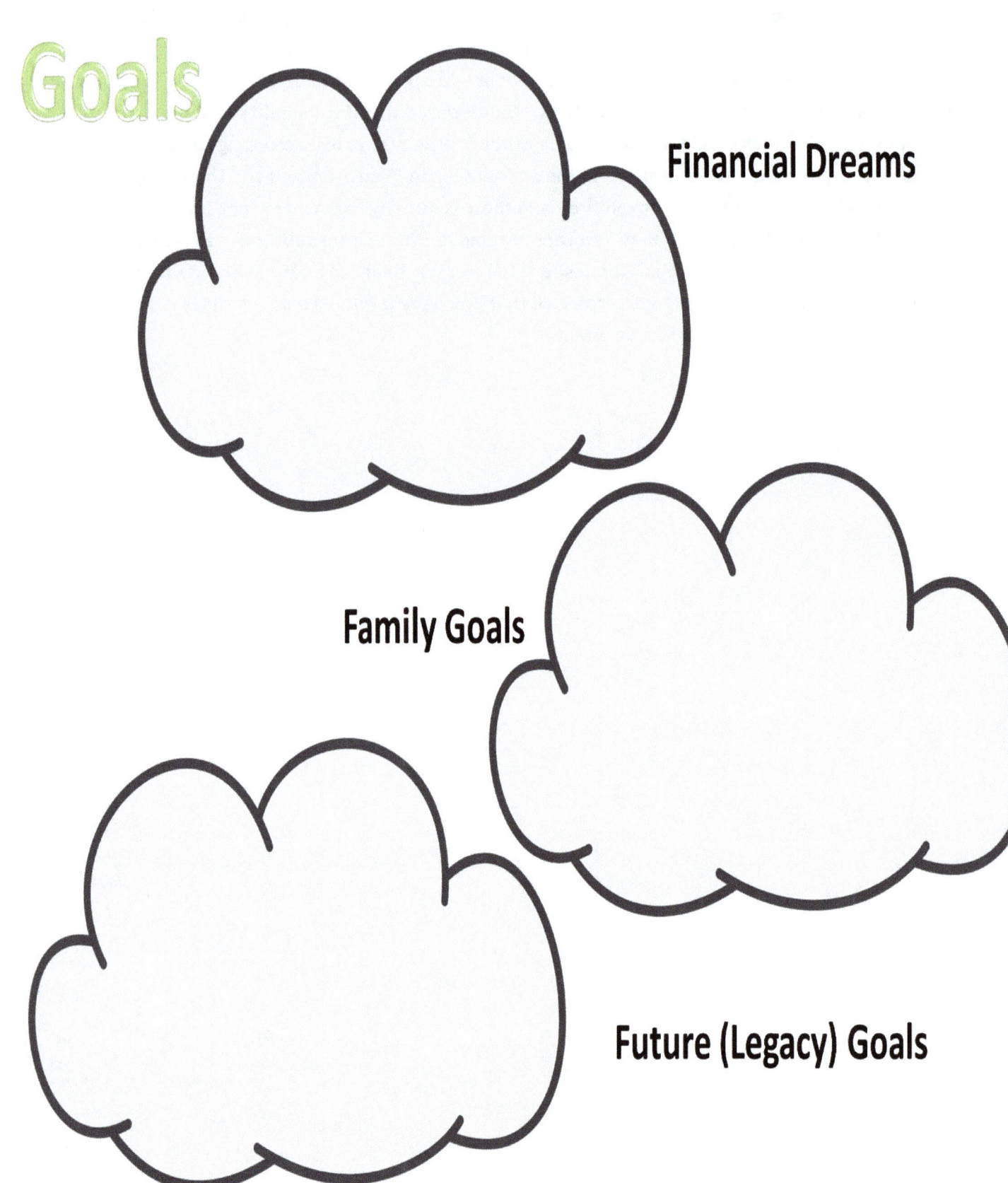

Financial Dreams

Family Goals

Future (Legacy) Goals

Examples include:

Financial Dreams –

- ❖ Stop creditors from calling
- ❖ Not have financial stress
- ❖ Pay family members back
- ❖ Handle my finances effectively
- ❖ Improve credit score to 750
- ❖ Be an example for others
- ❖ Be able to purchase a home for more space
- ❖ Help myself and my family change our path
- ❖ Give to ministries I believe in
- ❖ Have money work for me
- ❖ Retire comfortably

Family Goals –

- ❖ Have savings for children's field trips and extra curricula activities
- ❖ Lessons for kids – music and sports
- ❖ Once a year big vacation
- ❖ Pay for college for my kids
- ❖ Buy new car for my wife
- ❖ Family vacation to Australia
- ❖ Buy anniversary ring for my wife
- ❖ Buy golf clubs for my husband
- ❖ Travel for the holidays

Future Legacy Goals-

- ❖ Have a family owned business to pass down to my children and their children
- ❖ Leave a legacy of financial independence for my family
- ❖ Leave enough to pay for my funeral expenses
- ❖ Leave money for my children and my grandchildren

Once you've documented your goals try to list them in order of importance. You'll create a check list of what you are accomplishing and its priority to you and your family.

Chapter 2: Banking/ Credit

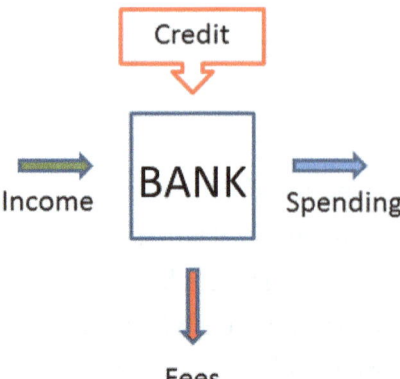

We begin our financial makeover deciding where to house the goods. Imagine a building that allows items to come in and the same going out. The building enlarges the more that comes in and it shrinks based on what goes out. In addition to the ins and outs there is also an entity that presses on the building from the top which can stretch the building. This entity is held up by a rod that is only released if you have more coming in than going out. When the rod is released the weight presses on the building and allows more to come out with less going in. That building is your bank and it needs to be managed if you are going to achieve the dreams you identified. The entity is your credit held by the rod of institutions that make the decision whether to lend to you or not and at what rate. It is important as we begin to understand how it all works together.

The first place to begin is where you keep your money. Typically under the mattress banking and savings is long outdated. However keeping up with your funds and wisely deciding where it is located takes a little effort. It is my opinion that you should not pay someone to hold your money. Banks use the money you deposit to lend to others and make money from your money. Monthly charges though they seem minor do add up.

> For instance, a $10/month service fee to maintain a checking account is equivalent to spending $120/year. That $120 can be used to pay down a debt, pay a utility bill for one month, buy a gift, etc. It's like having a pocket full of money with holes in it. Don't just give your money away; consider all fees and eliminate as many as possible. In other words, stitch up the holes.

Just as monthly fees should be reduced if not eliminated the same goes for late fees. If you pay on time (or early) you can avoid raking up additional charges. Paying a credit card or utility bill late can easily be and extra $100 or more a year. Late fees indicate that you are not paying attention nor have a plan in place to insure that what you owe is paid. Companies charge these fees not only to get more money but to insure that you give them what you owe them. As we go into budgeting we will discuss ways of putting the bills in a calendar and setting a schedule that will assist in timely payments. These late fees not only cost you money but also cost you points on your credit score. A poor credit score in turn costs you money with increased interest rates on any major purchase. Stop the bleeding from your accounts by paying on time.

As we turn our attention to the accounts that need to be set up it is a good idea to begin your research with a few sites that can help. Besides going to the individual bank websites for details, bankrate.com has calculators and will summarize institutions and their rates and requirements. It is a handy site for finance. Also don't forget to check your local credit union. If you meet the membership requirements, you may find them to have better rates, lower requirements, fewer fees and higher interest. Taking the time to research the bank will allow you to keep as much of your money as possible (interest rate).

Bank Accounts

It is necessary to research and set up the appropriate bank accounts. Let me say from the beginning that I don't believe you should pay anyone to hold your money. Banks use the money you deposit in order to lend to others and charge them interest. This said, the banks are making money on your money. What you will need to do is research. There are several accounts you will need to consider: checking, savings and money market.

A **checking account** is necessary to make payments for services and products you wish to purchase. What you will need to research is the minimum requirements; the interest rate; monthly charges; service fees; overdraft fees; etc. These items can easily be gathered from each banks website. There is also the opportunity to go to bankrate.com and get a summary of the best banks and their rates at that time. The minimum requirements would include the dollar amount that must be deposited, remain continually, or anything else identified by the bank. Usually this is required to avoid monthly service charges.

Checking Account
Purpose – Make payments for products and services

$_____

Minimum $ _____

Service fee: $ _____ ✗ eliminate

Overdraft fee: $ _____ ⬇

# of Transactions/month _____

Interest _____ % ⬆

Make sure you will be able to meet the requirements so that your account will not be in jeopardy. If the requirements are too stiff, then it isn't the right bank for you. Banks should earn the right to hold your money. Another item to verify is if the checking account is interest bearing.

In other words, will the bank give you a percentage of interest based on what monies you have in that account? This equates to free money or monies they are paying you to hold your money. Monthly service charges again I don't believe you should pay. There are several banks including credit unions that do not charge a service charge. Look at them first. If you must utilize a bank that includes a service charge, go for the lowest charge and usually this will be waived if the minimum requirement is met. Minimize this charge as much as possible. Overdraft fees only come into play if you overdraw or spend more than what is in your account. This should not be done if you are balancing your checkbook or keeping good records of what you are withdrawing. It is very important to verify the charges you make (debit card) or checks you write. If you don't add or subtract the dollars correctly you can end up with no money in your account. Just because you have checks left doesn't mean you have money. See the appendix for how to balance your checkbook. However, as you are doing research know what the fee entails. Is it a one-time charge per item or a daily charge until the account is brought up to the amount necessary? The better option is a per item charge and not a daily one. This can add up quickly. Also determine if there are any other service fees.

A quick word on debit cards verses writing checks. Debit cards take money immediately from your account. You will need a system that works for you to always keep track of what you have and what you have spent. Good recordkeeping is necessary. If you write checks, you can use a log or duplicates which allow you to document as you go. It is a good idea to use the same check registry log to document your debit card purchases. You will then be able to reconcile with the bank at the end of the month.

Savings accounts are used to hold money for a rainy day. They can be used to save for a large purchase, keep you from spending all you have, be a source of stability in case of unemployment, used as overdraft protection, or used for emergencies. This account should have considerably more interest attached where you can grow your money. The short term goal is to save a minimum of 3 – 6 months' salary (ideally these days this should be 6 -9 months of income). In case of unemployment this will allow you to live at the same level while you search for a new job. My recommendation though is if you are unemployed use much less in the event your job search is longer than expected. This savings after your minimum is reached can be used for large purchases such as a down payment or full payment of a car, deposit required for a new home, motorcycle, vacation, etc. You should dream big but have enough saved to enjoy your purchase. Treat this account as your intermediate savings. Make sure you research the requirements and any stipulations.

Savings Account
Purpose – Emergencies; large purchases; short term holding

$ _____

Minimum $ _____

# of Transactions/month _____

Interest _____ %

Goal: $ _____ (6 months of gross income)

Money market accounts are a source of receiving higher interest but the requirements for a minimum deposit is also higher. You will need to maintain that minimum amount deposited to avoid fees. In general, a money market account will also have limitations on the number of withdrawals you can make. In your research include identifying the stipulations. Once your savings reaches the minimum for the money market it is a good idea if you can work within the withdrawals to move most of your savings to your money market account

---

Money Market Account
Purpose – Mid to long holding

$ _____

Minimum $ _____

# of Transactions/month _____

Interest _____ %

Goal: $ _____

keeping a miscellaneous (discreet or smaller) amount in the general savings. This money market account when fully funded should ideally contain at least your 3 – 9 months gross income. It would remain liquid (doesn't require major actions to retrieve as necessary).

Online banking is also an option for checking, savings, money market and certificates of deposit (CDs). It is feasible to have both a local bank and an online bank. Generally the online banks will give you more interest; however, the delay to transfer the money is usually at least 3 days. Weigh out whether you can be structured enough to make a transaction in advance of your requirement for the funds to be available.

Basics of Credit

Credit scores are used by institutions to get a snapshot of how you handle your money. The higher your score in general the better you are perceived by banks, loan officers, mortgage lenders, etc. With that in mind you definitely want to have a great score because it can save you a lot of money. For example, why pay 18% interest on a loan with a poor credit score (550 or lower) when you can get 5% interest with a great score (680 or better). The difference can be enormous and is proportionate to the amount that you are borrowing [$10,000 loan for 3 years (36 months); @18% $361.52 monthly payment ($3014.86 interest); @5% $299.71 monthly payment ($789.52 interest)]. You could be paying 3 times as much to borrow just because you didn't understand credit and may have credit challenges with a low score.

So what's in a score?

There are several different scores but the 2 big ones are the FICO Score 8 and the Vantage Score 3.0. Scores range from 300 to 850. The FICO score is used by Discover card and takes into account your payment history, the amount owed and the percent you are using, the length of credit history, any new credit and inquiries, and the type of credit you have. The big 3 agencies Equifax, Experian and Transunion utilize Vantage and just identify it as your credit score. This method factors your card utilization percentage, payment history, age of your credit history, derogatory marks, total accounts and hard inquiries. The first step is knowing where you stand now. Check your score. One easy method is using a service like Credit Karma which is free. Some credit cards also give you a snapshot of your score with your bill.

"The wicked borrow and pay not again" – Psalm 37:21a

Payment history is a representation of how you pay your bills. Are you paying on time or are you late. If you have been late, how late are you 30, 60 or 90 days? The goal here is to be the sure bet that you will definitely repay whatever amount requested. Obviously who would want to lend money to someone who does not pay back the money? Would you? If you have been late in the past, contact the credit provider in writing or by phone to make arrangements to clear up those late indications and improve your credit score at the same time.

Amount owed and the percent being utilized is simply a reflection on whether you have maxed out your credit cards. If a company sets you up with a limit of $200, and you charge $100, then you owe $100 and your utilization is 50% (amount owed/ total limit X 100%). If you pay off that balance at the end of the month and the scores are calculated at that time your utilization is 0% which is excellent. What it says to the lender is that you pay your bills and you have room to get $200.

Length of credit history or age of credit history is calculated in months. The longer you have had a credit card the longer your length of credit history. Of course as you start out this category will be low but will increase with time. This is usually calculated by the card you have had the longest.

New credit and credit inquiries refer to you adding any additional cards and the limits they allow you to charge. The inquiries would be from the companies setting up the card. These inquiries don't stay on your account long but if too many are done at one time it can negatively affect your score.

The type of credit is an overall reflection on what you are spending your money on. If it is a revolving account which is department stores, major credit cards, etc. then it is everyday purchases. If the type of account is a mortgage then you have a long term debt for a house. Loans for cars, boats, education, etc. are listed as an intermediate term of debt. The more responsible you are the more you will have a combination of types of credit. These are weighed by the lender to determine if you can handle a new debt.

Derogatory marks are indications that you have failed in the past to pay your debt. This can be bankruptcy, foreclosures, collections, tax lien or civil judgments. These are long lasting negative reports that can last seven to ten years.

Hard inquiries are inquiries made by a financial institution as they check your credit for loans, mortgages, or credit with your permission. These usually stay on your credit report for two years. The good news is that it doesn't affect your score the entire time.

Improving Your Scores

The goal is to have your score to be 700 or better. 750 and greater is considered excellent. In order to start in this area you need to know your score and what is on your report. Annually you can request your credit report to check for errors. Ensure that the information on your credit report is correct and up to date. Several credit card companies and banks allow this at no charge. Federal law requires each of the 3 national consumer credit reporting companies give you a free credit report every 12 months if you ask for it. Beware of companies charging you monthly for this feature. Every 12 months you can get a copy of your credit report from each credit reporting company from annualcreditreport.com. Your score will change over the year but you may not need to check that often.

Review your credit score for any errors and report them to the company that has the error by opening a dispute. Contacting Experian, Equifax or Transunion isn't as daunting as you may think. Much of what you need to do can be done online (Experian.com/disputes/main.html; Equifax.com/personal/disputes; Transunion.com/credit-disputes/dispute-your-credit). You will need to prove that you are the one contacting them and they may require ID's to be scanned or faxed.

The easiest thing to do is to begin paying your bills on time and consistently. Setting up a schedule or signing up for automatic deductions can drastically improve your ability to stay on track. The appendix has a bill paying calendar template for you to use. Do not assume you have a grace period. If the bill is due on the 1st then make sure it is paid on or before the 1st. Companies are beginning to charge late fees immediately in order to make more money. Fees are like fleas, they bite. In addition, pay down balances as you can. Ideally your balances should be less than 30% of what you can borrow (% utilization). Some software or apps allow you to do "what if" calculations. This is making educated guesses on the improvement or detriment to your score if you make certain actions. Credit Karma and Discover will allow you to hypothesize on what would happen to your score if certain things were done. Some banks may also have this software. Using these should not stop you from paying down your debts.

When collection agencies call it can be unnerving! Sticking your head in the sand like an ostrich is not going to make them go away; you will need to deal with them. Calling creditors, negotiating balances to remove interest, and writing letters to eliminate debt if you are significantly in the hole is left for credit counselors and not discussed here. There are several reputable firms that aim to assist without creating additional hardships and hits to your credit score. Research again is key. Know your rights as a consumer, pay what you can, seek peaceful negotiations and agree with your adversaries quickly are all Biblical principles. The strongest admonition here is that in a multitude of counsel (godly) there is safety. Seek professional guidance. There are several quality companies that can help. A Right Way Credit Counseling (www.arightwaycreditcounseling.com) will assist without immediately damaging your current credit score. Another option may be financial counseling at your local church or www.H2HTruth.org.

Credit Score Highlight &Goals

	Goal
• Payment History: # of late payments ____	0
• Amount owed: _____ (this is your total debt)	$0
• % Utilization: _____ (Amount owed/Total limit x 100%)	0%
• Length of credit history: _____ (how long you have had credit)	The longer the better
• Derogatory marks: _____ Date to remove: _____	0
• Current Score _____	700+

Chapter 3: Budgeting

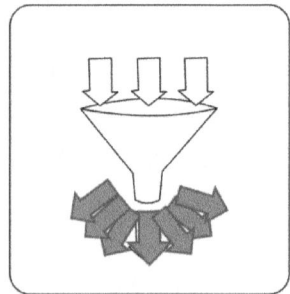

Now imagine a funnel. The opening at the top is wide but the bottom of this funnel looks more like an octopus. It has many legs. If there isn't enough coming into the top then the legs all don't get filled and some may even shrivel. Budgeting is managing this process. It takes looking carefully at all aspects in order to plug the holes and make it all work. Being realistic about what items will cost and ensuring that you are obedient to God's word so that you have Him in your corner is a must. Recognizing the difference between a need and a luxury is also a reality check that must be engaged. Simplifying and getting in touch with how you handle money will all be essential to working it out. We don't change anything we are unwilling to confront. The truth about self may hurt but telling yourself the truth is essential for improvement.

Budgeting is a way of identifying what is coming in and what is going out. If you don't have a budget you simply shoot from the hip. You have no clue of how to manage your money. It can be very easy to miss payments, always have to borrow, get into serious financial hardship and climb into a hole you can't get out. If you spend more than you make, the walls will eventually come tumbling down. There are several ways to set up a system but it is necessary to have a system that will work for you. The basic rule is to not spend more than you make. That sounds simple but often times the actual amounts being spent lie just below your conscience. Putting the numbers on paper brings a soberness that allows you to correct and adjust as needed. The simple rule of thumb is to spend some, save some and give some. Ideally, spend no more than 80% of what you bring in after taxes. Save a minimum of 10% of your income and give a minimum of 10% of your gross income (tithe). As you figure your budget and your spending lowers, increase your giving (offerings, missions, special requests, charitable donations, etc.) and savings.

'For it is He (God) that gives you the power to get wealth' – Deuteronomy 8:18b

The beginning of your budget starts with identifying how much you have coming in. This can be every 2 weeks, monthly or if you work on commission the numbers will vary. Calculate your gross income (income before any money is taken out). If you are paid weekly then multiply that number by 4; if you are paid every 2 weeks then multiply the number by 2; if you are paid on commission use your lowest income for the month. For example, you earn $10/hour and work a 30 hour week then you would make $300/week ($10 x 30) and you would have a gross income of $1200/month ($300 x 4). If you work on commission and have a base salary then use the base salary only for calculations. If your income is irregular but over the last year it varied from $2000/month - $4000/month then for budget purposes we will use $2000/month (the lowest payment). This will be our starting point.

Gross Monthly Income : _____

If you have more than one job or if you are married and your spouse works you will identify Salary 1 and Salary 2 separately using the same calculations listed above. In addition to salary you will include any investment income; stocks and bonds; and any other regular income. Your income category will look like this:

'If anyone will not work, neither should he eat' (2 Thessalonians 3:10) NKJV

Income:	Actual	Budgeted	Notes:
Salary 1			
Salary 2			
Investment			
Stocks and Bonds			
Alimony			
Child Support			
Other			
Total income			

The next step is to identify what you are deducting from that income or what you are spending. There are several categories that can be grouped as follows:

    Withholdings (Taxes, Social Security (FICA), health insurance, etc.)

    Finance Payments (Credit cards, loans, mortgages, etc.)

    Fixed Expenses (Insurances, cable, cell phone, utilities, tithes, etc.)

    Variable Expenses (Savings, donations, groceries, auto upkeep & gas, entertainment, etc.)

Take a look at a sample spreadsheet listing many of the items. These listings should be self-explanatory.

'Render unto Caesar the things which are Caesars' – Matthew 22:21			
Withholdings	**Actual**	**Budgeted**	**Notes:**
Federal Income Tax			
State Income Tax			
City Income Tax			
FICA			
Medical Insurance			
Dental Insurance			
Vision Insurance			
Health Savings Account (FSA/HSA)			
401(k)			
Total Withholdings:			

'Rich rule over the poor and the borrower is slave to the lender' – Proverbs 22:7			
Finance Payments	**Actual**	**Budgeted**	**Notes:**
Credit Card 1			
Credit Card 2			
Credit Card 3			
Credit Card 4			
Student Loan			
Auto Loan/ Car Payment			
Home Mortgage			
Personal Loan			
Total Finance Payments:			

'Seek first the Kingdom of God and all these things will be added unto you' – Matthew 6:33

Fixed Expenses:	Actual	Budgeted	Notes:
Tithes (10% of gross income)			
Rent			
Real Estate/ Other taxes/ HOA			
Auto Insurance			
Homeowners/ Renters Insurance			
Life Insurance			
Identity Theft			
Disability Insurance			
Long Term Care			
Cable/Internet/Phone			
Cell Phone			
Water			
Electricity			
Gas			
Garbage			
Total Fixed Expenses:			

'Honor the Lord with your substance and with the first fruits of all thy increase' – Proverbs 3:9

Variable Expenses:	Actual	Budgeted	Notes:
Offering			
Charitable Donations			
Emergency Fund			
Savings			
Groceries			
Auto repairs, tires, oil & gas			
Medications/ Co-pay/ etc.			
School/books/child care/sitter			
Furniture			
Clothing: Adults & Children			
Entertainment			
Dining Out/ Restaurant			
Gifts			
Vacation			
Memberships/ Subscriptions			
Pet Supplies			
Miscellaneous			
Total Variable Expenses:			

A few areas to pay attention to on your budget are groceries and dining out. Usually the original estimate for groceries is low. Increase this budgeted item above your initial thought. If you eat out regularly even if it is once per week it could significantly throw off your budget. Spending $10 on fast food once per week totals $40 per month. Dinner at a restaurant would be more significant. If you have a family of 4 (2 adults, 2 kids) and eat out, the bill can easily be $35 without a tip ($42 with a tip). That totals $140/month ($168/month with a tip) and that is significant.

As a beginning, put on paper the amounts you are spending in each category. Estimate the number if you are unsure. Make sure you estimate the grocery line item higher than you expect since this is typically a category that is usually underestimated. We will work with your numbers at this point but to be more accurate, I challenge you to document your spending over the next week as a starter, multiply by 4 and make the adjustments. Continue adjusting each listing until your income and expenses balance. Remember, you can't spend more than you make. Once you have everything budgeted and balanced you should work toward funding your emergency fund. When your 3 – 9 months of gross income is in your emergency fund, any excess cash can go to paying for your dreams and goals.

Envelope Method

For some, the idea of a spreadsheet and constantly referring to it is difficult throughout the month. I usually offer the envelope method for those who need to see in a tangible way their money allocations. What you will need is an envelope for each category listed. Make sure you put the envelopes in order of importance or by due date. As you get paid, put cash in each envelope at the beginning of the month if you are paid monthly. This will then represent what you have to spend that month and no more.

For example, your rent or mortgage will be the first envelope to be filled. Assume your rent is $600. As soon as you are paid you put $600 in the rent envelope. You would continue putting money in each envelope according to your budget. As the bills become due you use what you have to pay them. If for example you budget $75 for your water bill and this month it is only $50 then you have $25 additional remaining. This can either remain in the envelope in case you go over next month or be put in a miscellaneous envelope. Create a miscellaneous envelope to capture any variations in expenses or as a safety net for unexpected increases. The miscellaneous envelope money can be then redirected to savings/investing as you get closer to the end of the month. Miscellaneous is also good for unforeseen events that occur but keep in mind this should not be happening on a regular basis. Each month evaluate what is left over, what was short and adjust your budget appropriately. Remember to move toward a fully funded emergency fund of 3 – 9 months of gross (before taxes) income. Once this is achieved excess cash can then be used to pay for dreams, goals and investing for future gains.

God's Budget

According to the Bible it is important that we put our priorities in order. "**Where your treasure is there your heart will be also**"**(Matthew 6:21).** When you check your budget it will identify where you value your priorities. This will be reflected by the higher amount allocated to specific categories. You should not neglect your tithe (10% of gross income) in order to make your budget work. God should have preeminence. That's a fancy way of saying  He should have first priority in all areas of your life including your finances. After all, God gives us the power to get wealth (Deuteronomy 8:18b). As a covenant keeping child we can stand on His promises that He will rebuke the devourer for our sakes (Malachi 3:11). We can't ask for debt cancellation and believe it will happen if we are not acknowledging God in all that we do. It is important to note also that anything less than the 10% is not a tithe but a tip. Until the tithe is returned you are still in debt and it doesn't count in another category. God is not our cosmic bell hop where you put a dime in and expect $1000 to come out. Honor God and He will work with you to bless and do exceeding abundantly above all you could hope ask or think.

Obligations or vows we make to God requires that we pay (Deuteronomy 23:21, 23). With this in mind it is important to know what is in your budget and don't over extend yourself. There are many good projects (good ground) that you will probably like to sow into but are unable. Don't commit to any additional projects until you have completed your budget assessment. God requires that we count the cost before initiating a project (Luke 14:28; Proverbs 20:25). All this we will look into as we move into making your budget work (your financial game plan).

Finally, it is important to note that a good man (or woman) leaves an inheritance for his (or her) children's children (Proverbs 13:22). That means you should have room in your budget for savings and investing so that you can leave something for your posterity. Whether you started with funds given by your parents or not, now is the time to start a tradition that God ordained. Remember your legacy as you analyze your budget.

God's word gives us principles to follow for our good. Dr. David Jeremiah, Senior Pastor Shadow Mountain Community Church and founder of Turning Point Radio and Television Ministries in his book, *"The Coming Economic Armageddon: What the Bible warns about the New Global Economy"*, summarizes them as follows:

- **The Desire Principle**- Desire God above all else and don't try to serve two masters! (Matthew 6:19,21,24)
- **The Discernment Principle** – Learn the principle of contentment and honesty! (Proverbs 30:8,9)
- **The Discussion Principle** – Listen to wise counsel; don't act impulsively or foolishly! (Proverbs 19:20; 11:14)
- **The Discipline Principle** – Be faithful and deliberate; don't fall for get-rich-quick schemes! (Proverbs 28:20,22)
- **The Depreciation Principle**- Don't invest in things that are temporary; invest in things that will last for eternity! (Matthew 6:19-20)
- **The Due Diligence Principle** – Do your homework; count the costs! (Luke 14:28-29)
- **The Diversification Principle** – Invest in the future – your family and your descendants (Proverbs 13:22; 2 Corinthians 12:14; 1 Timothy 5:8)
- **The Devotion Principle** – Honor the Lord with everything you have and from the first fruits of your labor! (Proverbs 3:9-10; 2 Corinthians 9:7)

Your assignment is to meditate daily on these principles and Scriptural references and commit to obeying them (incorporating them into your life). (Joshua 1:8)

The goal is to be a good steward. A steward is defined as one to whose care is committed the management of the household. What we have belongs to God (Psalm 24:1). So how are you handling what God has given you? Your past assessment of handling money is not an indication of your future success. You can overcome and do better as you learn what that looks like. The road to better stewardship begins with God's plan in mind (Proverbs 3:9-10).

God's budget includes seven areas to review: tithes; offering; alms; savings; inheritance; necessities; and budgeting. As we move to becoming a better steward, continue to meditate daily on the following Scriptures related to these seven areas:

- **Tithes** – Malachi 3:9-12
- **Offering** – Exodus 25:1-8; Leviticus 1:1-3; Malachi 1:6-8
- **Alms (Charitable giving)** – Luke 6:34-35; Proverbs 19:17; Leviticus 25:35-37; 2 Corinthians 9:8; Luke 12:33; Proverbs 11:25; 1 John 3:17
- **Savings** – Proverbs 21:20
- **Inheritance** – Proverbs 13:22
- **Necessities** – Luke 12:22-34; Philippians 4:19; Matthew 6:25-34
- **Budgeting** – Luke 14:28-30

Financial Fitness Assessment

What is your financial fitness? The following assessment will indicate if you have warning signs, are headed for trouble, or are in serious trouble. Answer yes or no to the following questions.

1. Do you make only the minimum payment on your credit card and loan debts each month?
2. Are you at or over your credit limit on your credit cards?
3. Are you consistently juggling your bills each month and not paying all of them? Robbing Peter to pay Paul?
4. Do you often pay your bills late?
5. Are you robbing God by not paying your tithe?
6. Do you avoid or put off doctor or dentist visits because you can't afford them?
7. Are you dipping into your savings each month to cover expenses?
8. Are collection agencies calling you regarding an overdue bill?
9. Have you committed to a second job or overtime in order to make ends meet?
10. Are you unable to save or invest because there is more month than money?
11. Do you worry about money a lot?
12. Are you not eating properly (limiting food) because of you don't have the money?
13. Are you borrowing money regularly from family, friends, or payday express?
14. Are you taking items to the pawn shop to get money to keep your lights on?
15. Have any of your utilities been cut off in the last 3 months?
16. Is your credit card debt greater than 10% of your net income (income after taxes)?
17. Do you have less than 1 month income in savings?
18. Are you stressed about your financial future?
19. If you are married and you or your spouse lost your job would you be in trouble financially this month?
20. If you are married, do you and your spouse fight about money?

If you answered yes to 1 or 2 questions take this a warning sign. If you answered yes to 3 – 5 questions you have trouble that needs to be addressed immediately. Develop your budget, financial game plan, savings plan, and get out of debt plan. If you answered yes to more than 5 questions, you are in serious trouble and may need outside assistance.

Financial Game Plan

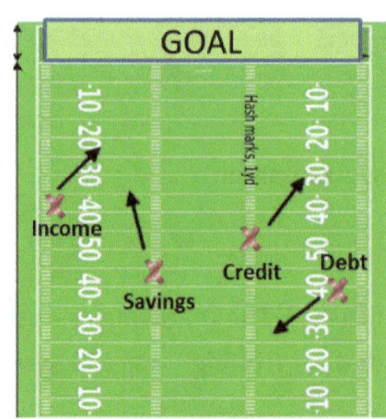

Once your budget is complete your income and expenses should balance. In other words, you should not be spending more than you take in. In order to get your financial house in order, what will it take? Stop living above your means! Your whole household must become frugal or you will be working against each other. A house divided against itself cannot stand (Matthew 12:25). Stop focusing on looking good instead of paying current obligations. Have a financial game plan and have a spending plan.

John 10:10 states Jesus came and died that we might have an abundant life. That is not for when you get to heaven but for the right now. You can achieve that by knowing what you have and who you owe. You must make intelligent decisions and effectively manage your resources. Devising a plan to put God's gifts to good use is the goal for this section. Our general rule is to spend some, save some and sow (give) some.

- Income – Deuteronomy 8:18; Proverbs 13:11
- Spend some – Luke 14:28
- Save some – Proverbs 13:22
- Sow some – 1 John 3:17

You work hard and your income should support you, your family and a comfortable lifestyle. Know that God blesses your hands (Deuteronomy 2:7). If you work on commission, pray and ask for favor with customers. Pray for financial increase in the area of your salary as well. Do your part but expect favor at your place of employment. Pray for your attitude to be one of excellence and ask for promotion. God is able to bring to you all that is needed.

Spending on fixed and variable items as listed in the spread sheet is necessary. Become a wise spender. Evaluate what you are spending money on and determine what is a necessity (food, clothes & shelter) and what is a luxury (cable, gym membership, grooming, shopping, entertainment, etc.). Your first priority is to make sure all your needs are met. Anything outside of that should be available to trim, cut or eliminate. In the multitude of counsel there is safety (Proverbs 11:14b), if needed ask for wise counsel to look at your spending and offer suggestions. Wise counsel may include financial counselors at your church or outside companies. Examine everything and leave no category untouched.

Saving is important! At this point just remember to start somewhere and be consistent. In the next section we will look at several options to begin. Commit to doing something at this point. Your savings goal should be 3 – 6 months of your gross income for emergencies. Don't despair if you are not there yet. Pray for God's help and trust that He will help you get there. Begin by paying yourself first after your taxes and your tithes. Even if you start with a dollar, commit to save something regularly.

Sowing or giving is the last area that comprises the financial game plan. This area includes your tithes, offerings, and charitable donations. Check your attitude about money and pray for a heart of compassion toward others. Develop a heart of a giver and actively seek others to bless. God loves a cheerful giver (2 Corinthians 9:7). If at this point your budget is tight, know that there are other ways to give (donations, time, service, etc.) but don't under any circumstance neglect your tithe. Always have God in your corner!

Spending Plan

Turning our attention to spending, let's critically look at your fixed and variable expenses. The goal should be to spend only a certain percentage in each area. A rule of thumb is 25% on housing (rent or mortgage including insurance); 25% on utilities, food, necessities, emergencies; 25% on taxes; and 25% savings, tithes, offering, investing & debt payments. Of course these can vary greatly. Since the categories listed previously don't line up exactly, let's identify key areas to review:

Category	Percentage
Housing (rent/mortgage & insurance)	25%
Charitable giving (tithes/offering/donations)	10 – 15%
Utilities (water/gas/electric/garbage)	5 – 10%
Food (groceries & dining out)	5 – 15%
Transportation (car payments, repairs, gas, etc.)	10 – 15%
Medical	5 – 10%
Clothing	2 – 7%
Savings/Investing	5 – 10%
Debt payments	5 – 10%
Personal/ Entertainment	5 – 10%

If any of the above listed categories are out of line with your budget, it is an indication that this is an area that needs your attention. Consider examining with the utility company what can be done to lower your bill. You may have a leak, water heater that needs insulating, a change in thermostat reading, etc. Beware of load leveling plans which tend to cost more because you don't see the fluctuation in the bill. The debt payment area is a significant one to examine. We will deal with debt reduction in a later section but this is a cause for much financial stress. If you are unable to save and invest, then Houston we have a problem. The goal is abundant life now; the only way to get to that point is balance and that means getting out of debt and freeing up funds for the future and fun.

Ecclesiastes 5:18 -20 NIV – *"Then I realized that it is good and proper for a man to eat and drink, and to find satisfaction in his toilsome labor under the sun during the few days of life God has given him—for this is his lot. Moreover, when God gives any man wealth and possessions, and enables him to enjoy them, to accept his lot and be happy in his work—this is a gift of God. He seldom reflects on the days of his life, because God keeps him occupied with gladness of heart."*

Now it is your turn to make the calculations and highlight the areas that require attention. Seek out simple ways to cut back and seek the assistance of wise counsel if necessary. There are several calculators online that will help with budgeting as well as apps through several banks at no charge. There are also great and reliable online guidance and professional help. See the Appendix for websites that may be of help.

As a reminder, God wants to bless you but can't if you are lacking in any area. You must have income so He can multiply it. You also must give so He can increase and bless you. Now is the time to make good spending decisions so there is something to prosper.

Chapter 4: Saving/ Debt Reduction

Savings Plan

As we've discussed, living paycheck to paycheck is a time bomb waiting to happen. So what do you do if you don't have 3 -6 months worth of gross income in some savings vehicle? Begin by saving now! There are several ways to start but I would suggest you first attack your budget and see what is available to cut so you can reallocate it to savings. Have a yard sale and get money for those material things you bought to keep up with the Jones'. Clean out your attic, sell the things you no longer need or want, and your savings has begun. See the Appendix for websites and apps to use to help you save. As you free up monies from the budgeted categories because of savings, put that in your savings account. If you are using the envelope method, gather all that is left over at the end of the month and this is your savings. If you are up to your eyeballs in debt and are spending everything on credit cards; once a card is paid off begin your savings. The goal is to start saving. Start with a small amount, grow from there, until saving becomes a habit.

Another way to save is by doing the popular 52 week money challenge. Every week of the year you save a specific amount and at the end of the year you will have saved $1378 not including any interest Here's the table showing your deposit and your account balance:

52 Week Money Challenge

Week	Deposit Amount	Account Balance	Week	Deposit Amount	Account Balance
1	1.00	$1.00	27	27.00	$378.00
2	2.00	$3.00	28	28.00	$406.00
3	3.00	$6.00	29	29.00	$435.00
4	4.00	$10.00	30	30.00	$465.00
5	5.00	$15.00	31	31.00	$496.00
6	6.00	$21.00	32	32.00	$528.00
7	7.00	$28.00	33	33.00	$561.00
8	8.00	$36.00	34	34.00	$595.00
9	9.00	$45.00	35	35.00	$630.00
10	10.00	$55.00	36	36.00	$666.00
11	11.00	$66.00	37	37.00	$703.00
12	12.00	$78.00	38	38.00	$741.00
13	13.00	$91.00	39	39.00	$780.00
14	14.00	$105.00	40	40.00	$820.00
15	15.00	$120.00	41	41.00	$861.00
16	16.00	$136.00	42	42.00	$903.00
17	17.00	$153.00	43	43.00	$946.00
18	18.00	$171.00	44	44.00	$990.00
19	19.00	$190.00	45	45.00	$1,035.00
20	20.00	$210.00	46	46.00	$1,081.00
21	21.00	$231.00	47	47.00	$1,128.00
22	22.00	$253.00	48	48.00	$1,176.00
23	23.00	$276.00	49	49.00	$1,225.00
24	24.00	$300.00	50	50.00	$1,275.00
25	25.00	$325.00	51	51.00	$1,326.00
26	26.00	$351.00	52	52.00	$1,378.00

Though you can follow the table each week for the year, I suggest you use it like bingo and put in the maximum you have that week. For instance, though it may be the 1st week of the year but you received an unexpected gift of $50 then put in the $50 and mark that week as complete. If you have enough to cover more than one of the weeks at the higher level, then do so. This means with interest you can save more. This also allows you to work backwards and when the end of the year comes you won't feel strapped about saving $52 that week, instead you will only need $1. The options are many: start at $1 and each week save the designated amount; begin at the end of the chart and work backwards; or use the chart like bingo and deposit the maximum you have available. Either way at the end of the year you have an emergency fund and the beginning of an established savings account.

52 Week Bingo Savings

FREE	29	32	16	4	24	18	8	31
9	43	5	23	38	7	1	41	3
42	15	27	52	47	49	28	22	34
25	37	19	46	FREE	45	26	19	29
11	13	35	50	48	51	14	44	2
33	39	21	39	17	12	36	6	40

Many financial professionals suggest 3 – 6 months of income should be the goal for savings. With the current economy and the length of time it takes to obtain another job, I would suggest 6 -9 months as a goal. Though this may seem out of reach at the time, keep working toward it. If this is secured in the most profitable location (highest interest rate bank account) then it will grow. As you pay off your debt and learn to operate wisely, you will achieve your goal and begin investing for your future.

Debt's Dilemma

Let's talk about the ball and chain of debt. The Bible declares that the rich rule and the borrower is slave to the lender (Proverbs 22:7). When you have debt (and most of us do in some form) you become a slave to the institution you owe. Yes, slavery is alive and well in the U.S. in the areas of finances. If you have a mortgage, until you pay it off you are living in a home that is really owned by the bank. Try not paying for a few months and they decide to foreclose, you will end up on the street without a home. So in effect, it's not yours until it is paid in full. The same goes for your car. Many a vehicle has been re-possessed because of lack of payment. You owe, you owe so off to work you go. The reason many people work is because of debts that need to be paid and it isn't at a job they enjoy. Some even get a second job to cover payments above their income. Now that is not abundant living!!

Let's look at some numbers when it comes to debt. The object here is to make debt so detestable to you that you will get out of it as quickly as possible and run from it in the future.

> Imagine you have 4 credit cards each carrying a balance and each requiring a minimum payment of $50. If you only pay the minimum you will be shelling out $200 each month in credit card payments alone. Worst yet, the balances are not going down $50 but if you look closely at your monthly statements, it may even be going up depending on your interest rate. Now use the actual number of credit cards you own and watch that monthly amount rise significantly to a point where the collection agencies are calling when you can't pay the minimum. This is financial stress.

Why are the credit card companies, department stores and every bank trying to get you approved for one of their cards? The answer is simple; they will make a ton of money off of you! The typical credit card interest rate is 21%. The typical department store card interest rate is 23%. The 'buy here 90 day same as cash' interest rate is 33% or more. No bank will give you anywhere close to 33% interest on your savings or money market account. They are in business to make money and it is your money they are after. So how much do they make based on the interest rates? Here are some examples:

If your balance on a card is $200 at 21% interest and the minimum payment is $10/month it will take you 24 months to pay it off or $240. That's 2 years of debt and $40 of interest.

If your balance is $1000 at 23% interest and your minimum payment is $25/month it will take 74 months to pay it off for a total of $1850. You just gave away $850!

If you bought furniture on the 90 day same as cash plan but you didn't pay off the $1500 in the 90 days ($500/month). Your interest rate is 33% from day one (~ $40/month).

Payday loans – Short term loans from a company that advances you based on you paying it back from your next paycheck (~ 30 days). The fees vary from $15 - $35 for each $100 borrowed. Consider the fee as you giving away money today that you don't have for tomorrow. $100 costs you $135 and it must be returned in a short time.

Tax advance or tax anticipation loan – Though these vary, having a company advance you funds based on your refund could be very costly. For example, one company charges a $50 fee and 36% interest which is equivalent to $80 for a 15 day loan of $2000.

Rent-A-Center – Sounds easy and convenient but can be very costly. For example a refrigerator may cost $36.99/week. You would pay $2922.21 for the rental fee but the retail value was $1221.51. That means the rental fee was $1700.70. That's more than twice the price.

Convenience Stores – You have the ability to run into them and pick up a quick item while you are at the gas station. They make it convenient yet they charge you for the convenience. They average 11% more than traditional grocery stores.

Pawn shops - These stores make collateral based loans to you. The term is usually 1 – 4 months and the fee is 5% -25%/ month plus a 20%/month service charge. If you don't return or lose your ticket, the item belongs to them.

Credit card companies made over $155 billion dollars in 2011!!

As you can see the companies with credit cards are in the business of making money. Your money! Beware of scams and any debt you can't pay off in the time allocated (at the end of every month for most cards or within the 90 days if same as cash, etc.)

Reducing Debt

The goal is to be debt free! That feeling of being free to do what you want when you want and not being anxious about how much it will cost; being free to pick up and go at any moment is true freedom. In order to reduce your debt there must be a plan. There are also several systematic approaches that when instituted can reduce your debt quicker.

Debt Snowball

Credit card debt is one of the major debts carried by most individuals. It is also one of the largest interest rates being carried which means you are paying quite a bit more than the original purchase price.

The first step is to know what you owe (total balance); minimum payment required; and interest rate. The aim for the debt snowball is to put your debt in order of what you plan on paying off. As you pay off one debt then the amount used to pay that one will be added to the amount you pay on the second card or loan. Your amounts being paid on the financial obligation keeps getting larger which allows you to systematically pay off all your debt. Here's what it will look like:

Credit Card 1 balance $300 minimum payment $25   18% interest

Credit Card 2 balance $1000 minimum payment $75   21% interest

Credit Card 3 balance $1200 minimum payment $50   15% interest

Credit Card 4 balance $2900 minimum payment $95   18% interest

Auto loan   balance $12,000 $275/month   6% interest   matures in 32 months

Mortgage   balance $230,000 $900/month   4% interest   matures in 15 years

Plan: Budget available $1450; Minimum total $1420; extra $30 to add to payment (from miscellaneous or unallocated)

1) Pay $55 on Credit Card 1 and minimum payment on all others until Credit Card 1 is paid off (about 7 months)
2) Pay $130 ($75+$55) on Credit Card 2 until Credit Card 2 is paid off (about 1 year)
3) Pay $180 on Credit Card 3 ($130 + $50) until paid off (about 1 ½ years)
4) Pay $275 ($189 +95) until paid off (about 2 years).

The auto loan would be next. Take the $275 you had been paying on individual cards and add to the auto loan. In other words, you can make double payments. Instead of 32 months and at this point you are down to 8 months. Paying double you then reduce you to 4 months.

The mortgage loan is the largest. One way to keep your mind off it would be to just keep paying and periodically check the balance. With 13 years remaining, sign up with the lender to make payments every two weeks (verify there isn't a fee). Though you are paying the same amount, because the interest is compounded daily the overall interest paid on the loan goes down significantly. You will with this method pay one extra payment per year ($900).

Mortgage calculators are very useful to determine what to do and when the debt will be satisfied. You can also do the "what if" scenarios. This can be started immediately. Also check your mortgage to determine if you are making PMI (Private Mortgage Insurance) payments which is added by the lender to insure you pay the mortgage. Usually when you have 20% of the loan paid you can request that portion be removed which will then change how quickly you can pay off the loan. Once this is the only debt remaining, the total of $275/month can be added to extra principle on one month. Before you know it, the debt will be paid off. If you had been struggling to save for emergencies then part of the $275 can be put into savings as you continue chipping away at the debt.

The snowball is designed to go from one debt to the other until it is all paid. You can select the lowest debt card and get short term gratification by seeing that debt eliminated. Another option can be to order the debts according to the interest rates from highest to lowest. Pay the higher interest card off first which allows you less in finance charges overall.

Make sure you are able to make all the minimum payments. If this is unreasonable then consolidating to a lower interest rate card may assist. This will then make your minimum payments lower and manageable. That is instead of four credit cards with a minimum total payment of $245; you can transfer to one card with a minimum payment of $150. There usually is a transfer fee so any loan in place should be evaluated to determine if the interest rates are too high and have dropped. New loans may require closing fees and new credit card transfers may require transfer fees. If you are unable to make these decisions yourself or feel uncomfortable, seek wise counsel. Again, seek out financial counseling at your church or a company that offers assistance without damaging your credit score.

Debt Snowball   The wicked borrow and do not repay – Psalm 37:21

Company	Debt owed	Interest Rate	Term of Loan	Minimum Payment	Amount Paying
1.					
2.					
3.					
4.					
5.					

Chapter 5: Investing/ Net Worth

Investing Basics

One reason for investing is to gain more interest on your money and secure your future. This is also used to leave an inheritance for your children's children (Proverbs 13:22). All monies used for investment should be anything you can afford to lose. Of course you don't plan to lose it but you won't be getting the monies you invest out anytime soon. This is for long term goals and planning. If you consider your vision; savings would be close up, more like your glasses; you would need binoculars for your investing. This in no way suggests you not keep an eye on your investments. Don't make the mistake of setting it and forgetting it. It is important to periodically check what is happening with your investments but you shouldn't stress about it daily.

Whether you have your savings and emergency funds already set or not, if you work for a major company that offers a 401(K) savings plan whether they match funds or not, take advantage of the opportunity. What this retirement plan does for you is to allow you to do an automatic deduction based on a percentage. You begin investing without thinking about it (automatically). Out of sight is out of mind and before you know it you will have a nice nest egg. If your company offers  matching funds then you hit the jackpot (contact the Human Resources department to find out more). Contribute as much as you can but at minimum maximize their matching contribution (i.e. If they match up to 5% then at minimum you contribute 5% which would equal a total of 10%).

The key to investing is to think of it as if you are looking through binoculars. It is for long term savings you invest for future gains. The goal is to reach your desired level of income for retirement (through 401 (k) or IRA investments) and to pay for dreams and goals (stock, bonds, mutual funds, CD's). The plan is not to touch the money invested for retirement until your 60's or 70's. You can have an investment account earmarked for college for your kids some 20 years down the road (see 529 savings plans or other options) but they should be in a separate account.

Here are some investment accounts to consider:

Retirement: 401(K); Individual Retirement Account (IRA) both traditional and ROTH; Target Date Funds, etc.

College: 529 College Savings and Prepaid Tuition; Coverdells and Custodial Accounts; Savings Bonds, etc.

General: Certificate of Deposit (CD); Mutual Funds; Money Market; Stocks; Bonds, etc.

There are many books on the market for investing (see financial websites listed in the appendix). It is good to get the terminology down and have a clear understanding of what is available and the advantages and disadvantages of each. This book isn't going to cover the ins and outs of investing only the minimum basics to get you thinking. If you are ready for the investing phase, **CONGRATULATIONS**!! The sooner you start the better the compounding. I would recommend getting books specifically on investing. With the multitude of options, it is beyond the scope of this book.

Net Worth Calculations

So, what are you worth?

Yes, you are priceless and truly Jesus thought you were to die for but let's put it on paper. The net worth calculation is simply taking your assets (what you own) minus your liabilities (what you owe). This calculation would need to include everything and can be as simple as the money you have in the bank subtracting the money you owe in loans that need to be paid back.

What should your net worth be? Multiply your age times your pre-tax household income from all sources except any inheritances and divide by 10

(Age x Pre-Tax Annual Income/ 10 = Net Worth)

Sample: 42 years old x $50,000 / 10 = $210,000

This is what your net worth should be. Given your age and your income, how does your net worth compare? If your net worth is equivalent or higher, you are an accumulator of wealth. If your net worth is lower, it is time to get your financial house in order! Plan now to increase your net worth later (increase income, reduce debt, increase assets, eliminate liabilities).

Here's a Net Worth spreadsheet to work through:

NET WORTH

Assets:
Cash & Checking Account
Money Market Account
CDs and Savings Account
Mutual Funds
Stocks and Bonds
Cash Surrender/ Life Insurance
Real Estate
IRA / 401(k)
Business Ownership Interest
Vested Pension
Home
Automobile
Clothing/ Jewelry etc.
Other Investment
Other Investment
Total Assets:

Liabilities:
Rent/ Mortgage
Charge Accounts
Student Loan
Automotive/ Personal loan
Insurance Premiums
Taxes
Other Debt
Total Liabilities

Net Worth (Total Assets - Total Liabilities)

Conclusion and Next Steps

Congratulations!! If you made it to this point and have worked through all of the tables then you have in hand a budget and a plan for saving. The goal was to get you to understand money and then devise a plan for you to use it wisely as a good steward. You are well on your way. You know how much you have coming in and you are planning how you spend what you have. In order to make sure you get out of debt you are committed to not spend more than what is coming in. You have a plan to reduce your debt and improve your credit.

The next step would be to move to the investment phase. Make sure you review your budget periodically and keep your savings and retirement going on a schedule. When all the moving parts are working together, you can run with endurance. The race isn't won by the swift but by the one that endures to the end (Ecclesiastes 9:11b). Remember consistency counts far more than a fast start.

Thank you for allowing the truth of the word of God to direct you in your finances. Jesus said this is a little matter (Matthew 23:23; Luke 11:42) yet it is difficult for some to trust God in the area of money. Keep moving forward by increasing your net worth and sharing with others what you have learned.

APPENDIX

Online Calculators:

www.Bankrate.com

www.Greenpath.com/tools-and-tips/calculators/budget-percent.htm

Additional financial/investing websites:

www.Kiplinger.com

www.Smartmoney.com

www.Forbes.com

www.Daveramsey.com

www.Christianpf.com

www.Heyhoward.org

www.compass1.org

Savings sites:

Ebates (http://bit.ly/2vbpVMM)

www.Savingstar.com

www.Groupon.com

Living Social app

www.Restaurant.com

www.Coupons.com

www.SmartSource.com

www.PrintableGroceryCoupons.net

www.Plenticard.com

Walmart savings catcher (Walmart app)

www.Doughroller.net

www.Thesimpledollar.com

Credit Counseling Sites:

www.Arightwaycreditcounseling.com

Investment Sites:

www.Investmentterms.com

www.Moneymorning.com

Business Plan Templates:

www.Businessnewsdaily.com

Excel Budget Spreadsheet:

https://1drv.ms/x/s!AoP9PGGbnN1jdLzVIivrSe2z7HY

Financial Counseling:

www.H2HTruth.org

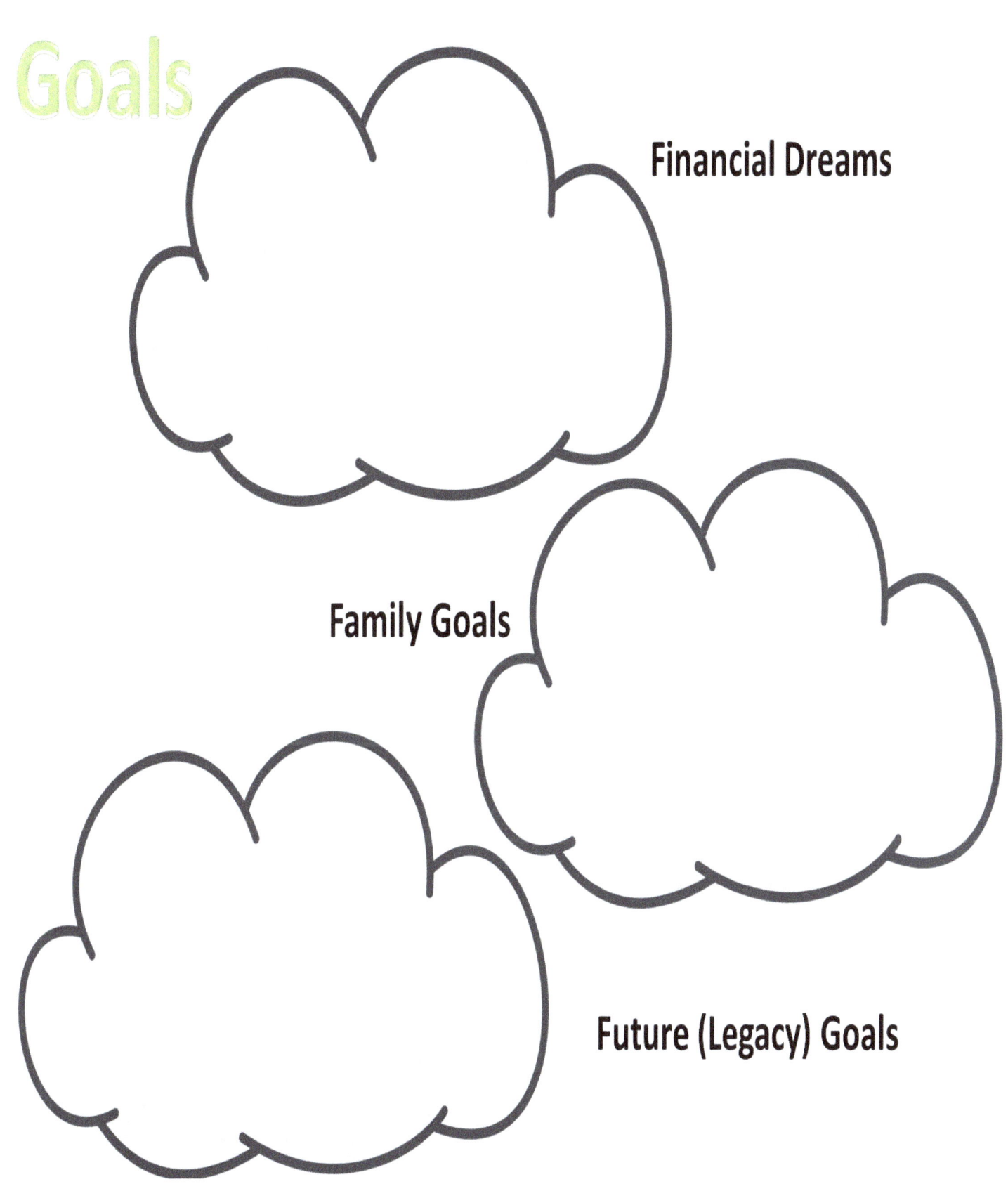

Goals (cont.)

Short Term

Savings _____

_____

_____

_____

_____

Debt Reduction

_____

_____

_____

_____

_____

_____

Credit Score

Long Term

_____

_____

_____

Investing _____

_____

_____

_____

_____

_____

BUDGET

Monthly Income: _____

Investment Income: _____

'Render unto Caesar the things which are Caesars' – Matthew 22:21			
Withholdings	**Actual**	**Budgeted**	**Notes:**
Federal Income Tax			
State Income Tax			
City Income Tax			
FICA			
Medical Insurance			
Dental Insurance			
Vision Insurance			
Health Savings Account (FSA/HSA)			
401(k)			
Total Withholdings:			

'Rich rule over the poor and the borrower is slave to the lender' – Proverbs 22:7			
Finance Payments	**Actual**	**Budgeted**	**Notes:**
Credit Card 1			
Credit Card 2			
Credit Card 3			
Credit Card 4			
Student Loan			
Auto Loan/ Car Payment			
Home Mortgage			
Personal Loan			
Total Finance Payments:			

'Seek first the Kingdom of God and all these things will be added unto you' – Matthew 6:33

Fixed Expenses:	Actual	Budgeted	Notes:
Tithes (10% of gross income)			
Rent			
Real Estate/ Other taxes/ HOA			
Auto Insurance			
Homeowners/ Renters Insurance			
Life Insurance			
Identity Theft			
Disability Insurance			
Long Term Care			
Cable/Internet/Phone			
Cell Phone			
Water			
Electricity			
Gas			
Garbage			
Total Fixed Expenses:			

'Honor the Lord with your substance and with the first fruits of all thy increase' – Proverbs 3:9

Variable Expenses:	Actual	Budgeted	Notes:
Offering			
Charitable Donations			
Emergency Fund			
Savings			
Groceries			
Auto repairs, tires, oil & gas			
Medications/ Co-pay/ etc.			
School/books/child care/sitter			
Furniture			
Clothing: Adults & Children			
Entertainment			
Dining Out/ Restaurant			
Gifts			
Vacation			
Memberships/ Subscriptions			
Pet Supplies			
Miscellaneous			
Total Variable Expenses:			

BILL PAYING CALENDAR

Month _____ **1st - 15th**

Bill	Amount owed	Due Date	Website/ Phone #	Automatic pay?

Month _____ **16th - 30th**

Bill	Amount owed	Due Date	Website/ Phone #	Automatic pay?

BALANCING YOUR CHECK BOOK

Beginning Balance:_____

Transaction	Date	Description	R	Withdrawl	Deposit	Balance

Purpose – To keep track of your money; catch mistakes; and avoid overdraft fees
1. Record all transactions as you make them: Additions (deposits or income) Subtractions (withdrawals or debits)
2. As you record, add or subtract from the balance as appropriate
3. When your bank statement comes in check off the transactions as they are recorded in the R column (reconcile)
4. Check your math!!
5. Don't forget any bank service charges (avoid these)!!

Transaction types: DEP (Deposit); ATM; EFT (Electronic Funds Transfer); Debit; XFR (Transfer); CHK # (Check); SVC (Service f

NET WORTH

Assets:
Cash & Checking Account
Money Market Account
CDs and Savings Account
Mutual Funds
Stocks and Bonds
Cash Surrender/ Life Insurance
Real Estate
IRA / 401(k)
Business Ownership Interest
Vested Pension
Home
Automobile
Clothing/ Jewelry etc.
Other Investment
Other Investment
Total Assets:

Liabilities:
Rent/ Mortgage
Charge Accounts
Student Loan
Automotive/ Personal loan
Insurance Premiums
Taxes
Other Debt
Total Liabilities

Net Worth (Total Assets - Total Liabilities)

Examples:

Monthly Income: $2,000   (Annual $24,000)
Investment Income: $5
Tax rate 15%   single   no children

	Actual
Federal Income Tax	300
State Income Tax	
City Income Tax	
FICA	
Medical Insurance	20
Dental Insurance	
Vision Insurance	
401(k)	5
Health Savings Account (FSA/HSA)	
Total Withholdings	**325**

'Rich rule over the poor and the borrower is slave to the lender' Proverbs 22:7

Finance Payments	Actual	Budgeted
Credit Card 1	50	
Credit Card 2		
Credit Card 3		
Credit Card 4		
Student loan		
Auto Loan/ Car Payment	200	
Home Mortgage		
Personal loan		
Total Finance Payments	**250**	

Fixed Expenses	Actual	Budgeted	Notes:
Tithes (10% of gross income)	200		
Rent	500		
Real Estate/Other taxes/ HOA			
Auto Insurance	60		
Homeowners/Renters Insurance			
Life Insurance	25		
Identity Theft			
Disability Insurance			
Long Term Care			
Cable/ internet/phone			
Cell phone	60		
Water	35		
Electricity	40		
Gas			
Garbage			
Total Fixed Expenses	**920**		

'Honor the Lord with your substance and with the first fruits of all thy increase' Proverbs 3:9

Variable Expenses	Actual	Budgeted
Offering	80	
Charitable Donations	10	
Emergency Fund	20	
Savings	20	
Groceries	310	
Auto repairs, tires, oil & gas	40	
Medications/Co-pay/etc.		
School/books/child care/ sitter		
Furniture		
Clothing : Adults & Children	15	
Entertainment		
Dining Out/Restaurant	10	
Gifts		
Vacation		
Memberships/Subscriptions		
Pet Supplies		
Miscellaneous	5	
Total Variable Expenses	**510**	

BUDGET

Monthly Income: $4,000   (Annual $48,000)

Investment Income: $10

Tax rate 27% married 2 children (1 school/1 daycare)

	Actual	Budgeted
Federal Income Tax	1080	
State Income Tax		
City Income Tax		
FICA		
Medical Insurance	30	
Dental Insurance		
Vision Insurance		
401(k)	10	
Health Savings Account (FSA/HSA)		
Total Withholdings	1120	

'Rich rule over the poor and the borrower is slave to the lender' Proverbs 22:7

Finance Payments	Actual	Budgeted
Credit Card 1	40	
Credit Card 2	40	
Credit Card 3		
Credit Card 4		
Student loan		
Auto Loan/ Car Payment	200	
Home Mortgage	700	
Personal loan		
Total Finance Payments	980	

Fixed Expenses	Actual	Budgeted	Notes:
Tithes (10% of gross income)	400		
Rent			
Real Estate/Other taxes/ HOA			
Auto Insurance	120		
Homeowners/Renters Insurance			
Life Insurance			
Identity Theft			
Disability Insurance			
Long Term Care			
Cable/ internet/phone			
Cell phone	90		
Water	40		
Electricity	60		
Gas			
Garbage			
Total Fixed Expenses	710		

'Honor the Lord with your substance and with the first fruits of all thy increase' Proverbs 3:9

Variable Expenses	Actual	Budgeted
Offering	150	
Charitable Donations	20	
Emergency Fund	40	
Savings	20	
Groceries	450	
Auto repairs, tires, oil & gas	90	
Medications/Co-pay/etc.	30	
School/books/child care/ sitter	320	
Furniture		
Clothing : Adults & Children	40	
Entertainment		
Dining Out/Restaurant	30	
Gifts		
Vacation		
Memberships/Subscriptions		
Pet Supplies		
Miscellaneous		
Total Variable Expenses	1190	

NET WORTH

Assets:	
Cash & Checking Account	275
Money Market Account	
CDs and Savings Account	2,000
Mutual Funds	
Stocks and Bonds	
Cash Surrender/ Life Insurance	
Real Estate	
IRA / 401(k)	10,000
Business Ownership Interest	
Vested Pension	5,000
Home	
Automobile	3,000
Clothing/ Jewelry etc.	1,000
Other Investment	500
Other Investment	
Total Assets:	**21,775**
Liabilities:	
Rent/ Mortgage	6,000
Charge Accounts	6,000
Student Loan	2,000
Automotive/ Personal loan	900
Insurance Premiums	240
Taxes	800
Other Debt	
Total Liabilities	**15,940**
Net Worth (Total Assets - Total Liabilities)	**$5835**

NET WORTH

Assets:

Cash & Checking Account	275
Money Market Account	
CDs and Savings Account	2,000
Mutual Funds	
Stocks and Bonds	
Cash Surrender/ Life Insurance	
Real Estate	
IRA / 401(k)	10,000
Business Ownership Interest	
Vested Pension	5,000
Home	140,000
Automobile	3,000
Clothing/ Jewelry etc.	2,000
Other Investment	2,000
Other Investment	
Total Assets:	**164,275**

Liabilities:

Rent/ Mortgage	110,000
Charge Accounts	4,000
Student Loan	1,000
Automotive/ Personal loan	900
Insurance Premiums	480
Taxes	2,000
Other Debt	
Total Liabilities	**118,380**

Net Worth (Total Assets - Total Liabilities) $45,895

Setting Goals:

It's not that hard to get the things you want in life if you start with well-stated goals that are:

- **Realistic** — Make the goal achievable so you won't get discouraged at the outset.
- **Appropriate** — Make the goal consistent with your lifestyle and expectations.
- **Time-specific** — Set a deadline for achievement to add urgency and motivation for action.
- **Measurable** — Include a target such as a dollar figure or timetable to measure your progress.
- **Challenging** — Make the goal attractive enough to pursue with excitement.

Sample Goal Statements:

- **Cash reserves** — To maintain cash reserves equal to a minimum of three months of current income for a total cash reserve this year of $12,000.
- **Education** — To save for four years of our child's education beginning in 2017 at an estimated cost of $21,000 per year in today's dollars.
- **Accumulation** — To save $26,000 within five years for a down payment on a house.
- **Retirement** — To retire and move to Florida in 20 years with an annual income of about $65,000 in today's dollars.
- **Tax management** — To contribute the maximum amount of pre-tax dollars allowable to my 401(k) each year.

Retirement instruments:

- 401(k)s
- Annuities
- IRAs
- Life Insurance
- Mutual Funds
- Pension Plans
- Privileged Assets Annuity
- Rollover IRAs
- Small Business Retirement Plans

Managing Debt and Credit
Key Points

Installment Debt
Debt comes in many forms, and most types help us in our daily lives — when used responsibly. Most people cannot buy a home without some financial help, and many cannot buy a car (especially a new one) without some sort of financing. The money borrowed to purchase large-ticket items is called installment debt: The debtor pays a portion of the total at regular intervals over a specified period of time. At the end of that time period, the loan with interest is paid off.

Revolving Credit
A revolving line of credit, also called "open-ended credit," is made available to you for use at any time. Examples of revolving credit are credit cards such as Visa, MasterCard, Discover, American Express, and department store cards. When you apply for one of these cards, you receive a credit limit based on your credit payment history and income. When you use the credit line, you must make monthly minimum payments based on the total balance outstanding that month. Some lines of credit will also have an annual account fee. Spending more than you earn in any given period is a dangerous practice at best, but doing it over an extended period of time can be financial suicide.

Use Credit Wisely
To use credit intelligently, start by examining the terms of the card(s) you are currently using. Keeping track of your cards, their rates, and your current balances will help you to be aware of how you use credit cards.

Eliminating Credit Card Debt
If you think you may have too much credit card debt, begin to address it by honestly evaluating your spending habits. Examine your existing expenses to analyze how your money is spent. You will most likely be able to identify the problem areas where you are more likely to spend too much or too readily with credit cards. Then, based on your current spending practices, create a realistic budget to pay off your credit card debt in the shortest time possible while not adding any more debt to it.

Points to Remember
Installment debt means the loan is paid off in a specified period of time by making predetermined payments periodically. Revolving credit is a line of credit that is instantly available through use of a credit card. As you pay down your debt in a revolving line of credit, the minimum payment is also reduced, thus extending your payoff period and, consequently, the interest you pay.

Spending more than you earn in any given period is a dangerous practice at best, but doing it over an extended period of time can be financial suicide.

Three Steps to Reduce Debt
Once you've got your budget settled, you can begin to attack your existing debt with the following steps:
Pay off high-rate debt first. The higher your interest rate, the more you wind up paying. Begin with your highest-rate credit cards and eliminate the balance as aggressively as possible. (Debt Avalanche method)
Transfer high-rate debt to lower-rate cards. Consolidating credit card debts to a single, lower-rate card saves more than postage and paperwork. It also saves in interest costs over the life of the loan. Comparison shop for the best rates, beware of "teaser" rates that start low, say, at 6%, then jump to much higher rates after the introductory period ends. However, '0%' interest cards can be beneficial. You can also contact your current credit card companies to inquire about consolidation and lower rates.

Borrow only for the long term. The best use of debt is to finance things that will gain in value, such as a home, an education, or big-ticket necessities, like a washing machine or a computer, that will still be around when the debt is paid off.

Maintaining a Good Credit Rating

Why Credit Is Important

It is important to establish credit if you plan to buy a home or automobile someday. Credit cards also provide a means of reserving a hotel room or obtaining cash while you're traveling.

If you are a college student, recent graduate, or a nonworking spouse, you can begin to establish credit by opening a savings or checking account in your own name. You can then apply for a department store and/or oil company credit card.

Creating a positive credit history for yourself requires using your credit card intelligently. Following are some dos and don'ts to help you manage credit effectively:

- DO NOT charge more than you can easily pay off in a month or two.
- DO NOT be fooled into paying just the low minimum amount listed on a bill. Credit card issuers make money on interest; there's nothing they'd like more than to have you stretch out payments.
- DO consistently pay your bills by the due date.
- DO use credit for larger, durable purchases you really need, rather than non-durables, such as restaurant meals that are better paid in cash.

Missing Payments

When you miss a payment, the information immediately goes into your credit report and affects your credit rating. If you're judged a poor credit risk, you may be refused a home mortgage or rejected for an apartment rental. In addition, a prospective employer looking for clues to your character may dismiss your job application if your credit report reflects an inability to manage your finances. In most states, an auto insurer may put you into its high-risk group and charge you 50% to 100% more if your credit record has been seriously blemished within the last five years. Many property insurers also review credit histories before they issue policies.

How Credit Reporting Works

The Fair Credit Reporting Act (FCRA), the federal statute that regulates credit bureaus, requires anyone who acquires your credit report to use it in a confidential manner.

The following information is most likely to appear in your credit report:

- Your name, address, social security number, and marital status. Your employer's name and address, and an estimate of your income may also be included.
- A list of parties who have requested your credit history in the last six months.
- A list of the charge cards and mortgages you have, how long you've had them, and their repayment terms.
- The maximum you're allowed to charge on each account; what you currently owe and when you last paid; how much is paid by the due date; the latest you've ever paid; and how many times you've been delinquent.
- Past accounts, paid in full, but are now closed.
- Repossessions, charge-offs for bills never paid, liens, bankruptcies, foreclosures, and court

judgments against you for money owed.
- Who owes the debt — you alone, you and a joint borrower, or you as cosigner. (Debts that you co-sign become part of your credit history, the same as debts you incur yourself.)
- Bill disputes.

Negative information can be kept in your file only for a limited time. Under the law, delinquent payments can be reported for no more than 7 years and bankruptcies for no longer than 10 years.

Credit Reporting Agencies

- **Equifax:** (800) 685-1111, www.equifax.com
- **Experian:** (888) 397-3742, www.experian.com/consumer
- **TransUnion:** (800) 888-4213, www.transunion.com

Be Smart with Credit

The FCRA entitles you to review information in your credit file. If you have been denied credit, the company denying credit must let you know and give you the name and address of the credit agency making the report. Once you have this information, you can send a letter to the agency and you will receive the information in your credit file, at no cost, within 30 days. It's a good idea to obtain a copy of your credit report to check it for accuracy. If you wish to dispute any information in your file, simply write the agency and ask them to verify it. Under the law, they are required to do so within a "reasonable time," usually 30 days. If the agency cannot verify the information, it must be deleted from your file.

What Is Bankruptcy?
Bankruptcy was created to protect the financial health of the jobless and the infirm by eliminating high levels of debt. There are two ways to file for bankruptcy, each with its own rules. The Bankruptcy Abuse Prevention and Consumer Protection Act of 2005 (Bankruptcy Reform Act), effective in October 2005, makes many changes in bankruptcy law.

Under a Chapter 7 bankruptcy filing, many debts are eliminated, but the filer must liquidate personal assets to pay down some of the debt. Personal property is sold by a bankruptcy trustee, who then uses the proceeds to pay creditors. Some assets are exempt if they are considered necessary to support the filer and any dependents, but state and federal laws vary widely. In general, a percentage of home equity and disability benefits are exempt, and Chapter 7 filers may be allowed to keep any money or property they obtain after filing. Chapter 7 bankruptcy can be filed once every eight years.

A Chapter 13 filing does not erase debt. Rather, it requires the filer to set up a repayment plan, typically over a three- to five-year period, in exchange for keeping personal assets. A reduction of debt is possible under a Chapter 13 filing, but payments to creditors must equal the minimum that would have been paid under a Chapter 7 filing. To qualify for Chapter 13, filers must have a steady income stream, unsecured debts (including credit cards) of less than $250,000, and secured debts (including mortgages) of less than $750,000. The Bankruptcy Reform Act, effective in October 2005, states that anyone with income above the state median will have to file for Chapter 13 and pay back at least a portion of their debts. In general, homes will only be protected if owned for at least 40 months. Chapter 13 bankruptcy can only be filed once every two years, effective in October 2005.

Certain debts cannot be erased under any bankruptcy filing, including alimony, child support, property settlements, criminal judgements and fines, student loans, and most taxes. In addition, a bankruptcy filing will not allow you to keep property that secures a loan, such as an automobile or home, unless you repay the loan.

Drawbacks to Bankruptcy

A bankruptcy filing is a black mark on your credit history. This can make it difficult to obtain loans, mortgages, and credit cards. Both a Chapter 7 and a Chapter 13 bankruptcy will appear on your credit report for 10 years. During this time, you may be subject to several financial hardships.

- **Secured loans may be more expensive to acquire.** Only a handful of lenders may approve you for mortgage and car loans. Acquiring a loan or mortgage may require an initial down payment of as much as 50%, and you may need to accept interest rates significantly higher than those offered to people with clean credit histories.
- **Unsecured loans may be impossible to acquire.**
- **Not all retirement account assets are protected.** Qualified retirement accounts, such as 401(k)s, are protected in all bankruptcy filings. And, as of October 2005, up to $1 million in an individual retirement account will be protected. Until then, the laws of the state where you file will determine whether your IRA assets are protected. Federal law requires that only those assets needed to support a filer and dependents are exempted, so you may only be able to keep a portion of an IRA account.
- **New legislation makes filing for bankruptcy more difficult.** The Bankruptcy Reform Act of 2005 (effective in October 2005) prohibits some people from filing for Chapter 7 bankruptcy; adds to the list of debts that people cannot get rid of in bankruptcy; makes it harder for people to come up with manageable repayment plans; and limits the protection from collection agencies for those who file for bankruptcy. In addition, anyone filing for Chapter 7 or Chapter 13 must undergo credit counseling at their expense six months prior to filing for bankruptcy and will also be required to take a financial-management course after filing.

Alternatives to Bankruptcy

Bankruptcy, and the resulting credit difficulties, is not the only way to manage excessive debt. You can try to negotiate a payment plan with a creditor and perhaps reduce your debt. Credit card companies faced with the rising number of bankruptcy filings may prefer to get some of what's owed them rather than have the entire debt erased.

Where to Turn for Help

Credit Counseling
A Right Way Credit Counseling (813-421-3522, www.arightwaycreditcounseling.com) – Services are personalized and will not damage your credit score.

Consumer Credit Counseling Service (800-388-2227, www.nfcc.org) — This organization has offices nationwide and charges a nominal fee or nothing for its counseling services.

General Information
Myvesta.org (800-680-3328, www.myvesta.org) — Formerly the Debt Counselors of America, this organization offers a variety of debt reduction materials, including free publications, debt-reduction packages, and credit report information.

The Institute of Consumer Financial Education (619-232-8811, www.financial-education-icfe.org) — Offers materials to help consumers manage their finances, including the *Do-It-Yourself Credit File Correction Guide*.

Source: Administrative Office of U.S. Courts.

Put Your Own Financial House in Order

Review your credit report to ensure that all information is correct. If you have past credit problems, don't lose hope. Be prepared to present a rationale for each slipup, and demonstrate an improvement in your ability to pay bills on time.

Mortgage Basics

How Much Mortgage Can You Afford?
The Federal National Mortgage Association (Fannie Mae) is a government-sponsored organization that purchases mortgages from lenders and sells them to investors. Two income-to-debt ratios established by Fannie Mae are standard requirements for conventional mortgages. The first requirement is that monthly mortgage principal and interest payments (P&I), plus insurance and property taxes, cannot exceed 28% of the buyer's gross monthly income (some exceptions may apply to increase this limit to 33%). The second requirement limits total monthly debt payments (housing, credit cards, car payments, etc.) to 36% of gross monthly income. In addition to these requirements, you may have to pay 10% to 20% down on the total purchase price to qualify for a conventional mortgage.

Source: National Association of Home Builders, Economics Division.

Types of Mortgages
How much house you can buy also depends on your mortgage's term and interest rate. The term is the length of time (usually 15 or 30 years) over which payments will be paid. The rate can be fixed (meaning it doesn't change over the

loan's term) or adjustable (it fluctuates with market conditions). Thirty-year fixed-rate mortgages remain the most popular. The longer term lowers the monthly payment, while the fixed rate provides stability over the life of the loan. Given relatively low interest rates, these mortgages are attractive to buyers planning to stay at least six or seven years in their new home. The drawbacks are low principal payments in the early years, and the risk that market rates will decline over the term. However, if your credit history is sound and you have sufficient income, you can usually refinance your mortgage when rates decline.

A 15-year term lowers the interest rate, reduces total interest payments, and increases principal payments. But it also increases monthly payments. If you can't afford the higher payments now, you might opt for a 30-year mortgage. If there are no prepayment penalties, you can make additional principal payments as your income increases. Making just one extra monthly payment a year will pay off a 30-year mortgage in less than 22 years and save tens of thousands of dollars in interest costs. If you plan to stay in a home no more than three years, you might want an adjustable-rate mortgage (ARM). ARMs offer initial rates that are lower than fixed mortgages. At some point, usually after the first year, rates are tied to market conditions and are subject to potential rate increases. Most ARMs include a cap on rate increases in any given year, as well as over the life of the loan. Some ARMs offer initial rates at least 2% below fixed rates and limit increases to 2% annually and 5% to 6% over the life of the loan. Many home buyers are attracted by the affordability of an ARM during the initial period. However, you should be confident that your future income will be sufficient if both interest rates and your monthly payments increase.

Another popular mortgage involves a balloon payment. A balloon is a lump-sum payment that pays off the loan in full after a fixed period of time. Generally the rates on balloon mortgages are 1/4% to 3/4% less than on 30-year fixed mortgages, but during an initial period of between 3 and 15 years, payments are similar. After this period, the remaining outstanding principal balance is either due in full or subject to refinancing. This is a good option for home buyers who plan to sell before the final payment is due. But because property values fluctuate, you may not be able to sell when you want. You may also face higher payments if you are forced to refinance at a higher rate, and there is also a risk that you may not be in a position to refinance when the balloon becomes due.

Interest Rate Points
Points are interest paid in advance to reduce the rate on a loan. One point is equal to 1% of the mortgage amount. The general rule is that 1 point is worth 1/8 of 1% off the loan rate. The decision to pay points for a lower rate is based on how much the seller is willing to contribute to points, how long you plan to stay in the house, and how important lower payments are vis-à-vis higher closing costs. You will need to calculate the long-term value of points based on these factors, keeping in mind that points are generally tax deductible in the year paid.

Other Alternatives

If you cannot afford a conventional mortgage, there are a variety of alternatives. An anxious seller will sometimes offer owner financing. Federal Housing Administration (FHA) loans offer down payments as low as 3%, but may require the buyer to purchase mortgage insurance. (The FHA is a government agency responsible for insuring affordable housing mortgages.) The Veterans Administration (VA) offers no-money-down mortgages to qualified veterans of the U.S. military. Finally, there are local affordable housing advocates that offer low-cost, low down-payment loan alternatives. For further information, contact the FHA, VA, Fannie Mae, or your local mortgage lender or real estate broker.

How Much Home Can You Afford?

Bob and Janet's combined income is $50,000 a year, or $4,166 a month. Their housing expense ratio of 28% yields a monthly maximum of $1,166 for mortgage, insurance, and taxes ($4,166 x 0.28 = $1,166).
Their total debt ceiling of 36% is $1,583 (4,166 x 0.36 = $1,500). Their monthly debt payments include a $200 car payment, credit card payments of $100, and student loan payments of $200. Subtracting this total of $500 from the $1,500 permitted leaves $1,000 in monthly housing payments.
Source: https://locktonlifegame.com/content/Buying_Your_First_Home.html

Calculators:

https://www.nerdwallet.com/mortgages/how-much-house-can-i-afford/calculate-affordability

http://www.bankrate.com/calculators/mortgages/new-house-calculator.aspx

Practical Financial Stewardship Study

Definition of Stewardship:

What we have belongs to _____. (Psalm 24:1)

How are you handling what God has given you?

Financial Fitness Checkup:

Road to better stewardship: Proverbs 3:9-10

_____
_____
_____
_____
_____

God's Budget includes 7 areas: (write out Scriptures)

Tithes: (Malachi 3:9-12)

_____
_____
_____
_____
_____
_____

Offering: (Exodus 25:1-8; Leviticus 1:1-3; Malachi 1:6-8)

_____
_____
_____
_____
_____
_____
_____
_____
_____

Alms: (Luke 6:34-35; Proverbs 19:17; Leviticus 25:35-37; 2 Corinthians 9:8; Luke 12:33; Proverbs 11:25; 1 John 3:17)

_____
_____
_____
_____
_____
_____
_____
_____
_____
_____
_____
_____
_____
_____
_____
_____

Savings: (Proverbs 21:20)

_____
_____

Inheritance: (Proverbs 13:22)

_____
_____

Necessities: (Luke 12:22-34; Philippians 4:19)

_____
_____
_____
_____

Budgeting: (Luke 14:28-30)

_____
_____
_____
_____
_____

Current vs. Better Steward

What will it take?

1. Stop living above your means!!
2. Your whole household must become frugal... you, spouse, children
3. Learn to say NO or not now.
4. Stop focusing on looking good: leads to second-rate economic achievement.
5. Have a Financial Game Plan
6. Have a Spending Plan

Action items:

_____
_____
_____
_____
_____
_____
_____
_____
_____
_____
_____
_____
_____
_____
_____
_____

Notes:

Financial Game Plan:

1. Get debt under control/ credit management:
2. Debt: Repay (Psalm 37:21; Leviticus 19:23; Exodus 22:14)
    a. Be willing to sacrifice to climb out of the hole you are in
    b. Stop ringing up new charges. Take the credit cards out of your purse/wallet
    c. Consolidate credit card debt to a lower interest rate card
    d. Know what you owe
    e. Double your payments
    f. Debt snowball system
    g. Owe not (Deuteronomy 15:6; 28:12, 44; Proverbs 22:7; Romans 13:8)
3. Pay on time – cut out late fees
4. Remove overdraft charges and bank fees
5. Reduce where you can:
    a. Auto insurance – re-evaluate
    b. Cell phone
    c. Cable
    d. Rent a center; Payday advance; Convenience stores
    e. Large $ items
    f. Overspending at holidays and birthdays
6. Save before purchasing cars/homes
7. Income Tax refunds – use half to pay off debts
8. Pay workers (Deuteronomy 24:10-17)
9. Co-signing: (Proverbs 6:1-5; 11:15; 17:18; 22:26)

Action items:

_____
_____
_____
_____
_____
_____
_____
_____
_____
_____
_____

Necessities vs. Luxuries

My needs:

_____
_____
_____
_____
_____
_____
_____
_____
_____
_____
_____
_____

My luxuries:

_____
_____
_____
_____
_____
_____
_____
_____
_____
_____
_____
_____

Spending Game Plan:

1. Income and Expenses analysis (budget)
2. Goal setting
3. Investing
4. Become an Entrepreneur:
    a. Business Idea – Service/Product
    b. Target Market (Customers) – Niche
    c. Business Plan – Key Players – Financial Solvency
5. Lending: (Luke 6:35; Deuteronomy 15:8; 23:19-20; Matthew 5:42; Proverbs 19:17)

Action items:
_____
_____
_____
_____
_____
_____
_____
_____
_____
_____
_____
_____
_____
_____
_____

Notes:

Dr. Chonta Haynes is a Theology and Christian Education professor at Grace & Truth Christian University where she also serves as the Academic Operations Officer developing curriculum and overseeing student affairs. She is active in leadership at her local church, The Word of Grace and Truth Ministries in Tampa Florida; serving as the coordinator for Jesus University (ages 3 -19), assisting in financial counseling for individuals and couples, ministering at the local hospital (Florida Hospital formerly University Community Hospital), and doing all as unto the Lord. Her outreach continues through her service to the community in her position as Chaplain with the Tampa Alumnae Chapter of Delta Sigma Theta Sorority, Inc. a public service sorority.

Dr. Haynes is uncompromising when it comes to the word of God. She has a caring heart that shows through her sensitive and logical approach to everyday issues. It was through her passion to help believers live an abundant life, Heart 2 Heart Truth Ministries was birthed to disseminate information in a multitude of forms to bless the body of Christ on a larger scale. From youth to money and everything in between she pours her heart into God's word seeking treasures to share with others. Her exciting, inviting, encouraging, fire cracker personality in Biblical teaching is galvanized in several works.

Dr. Haynes has been married for over 25 years and is blessed by the unwavering support of her husband. Through their union they have been blessed with three daughters, one of which awaits their heavenly arrival. Her family continues encouraging her authenticity, generosity, and active participation in reaching the masses for Christ.

Also available:

Family Worship: Reaching All Who Attend   ISBN 9781436370158
Not Just Paper   ISBN 9780999173336
Divinely Connected: Steps to Fearless Financial Freedom
                                            ISBN 9780999173343

Other Books, videos, online courses and coaching can also be found at

www.H2HTruth.org
www.linkedin.com/in/chonta-haynes

www.instagram.com/ctahaynes

www.pinterest.com/chontah/messages

www.facebook.com/chonta.haynes
www.facebook.com/h2htruth

www.twitter.com/chonta_haynes

Dr. Haynes gives great insight for those that desire to attain a stress free financial life. Beginning with the financial mind-set to the basics of investment, an easy to follow plan is laid out. This book will be a valuable treasure in anyone's financial literature library.

~ Dr. Thomas L. Dozier
President, Grace & Truth Christian University * Senior Pastor, The Word of Grace and Truth Ministries
www.graceandtruthempowered.org

The simplistic straight forward use of practical application is steeped in the richness of the Word applied to everyday practices. Dr. Haynes takes a thought provoking approach to everyday concerns with results that elevate the reader while engaging him. Transformative for individuals, families, communities and nations, if applied. The challenge for the reader is to be a doer of the Word to live a stress free abundant life.

~ Artricia James-Heard
Retired United States Navy Veteran * Owner, A Right Way Credit Counseling
Founder, A Right Way Foundation (a financial literacy not for profit organization)
www.arightwaycreditcounseling.com

Financial Coaching, Group workshops, Seminars, and Lectures can be scheduled at
https://H2HTruth.org

Notes:

www.ingramcontent.com/pod-product-compliance
Lightning Source LLC
Chambersburg PA
CBHW060426010526
44118CB00017B/2385